# Celebrities In Spirit

## AfterLife Wisdom for Mastery & Success

*by AthenaStar*

**Author Disclaimer**

The contents of this book are believed
to be from the interpretations and experiences
of AthenaStar based on interactive communication
with "Celebrities in Spirit." It is the author's intention to relay
messages of inspiration from "Celebrities in Spirit"
to the reader. There is no intention to malign
or cast aspersions on the personalities
in this book. This book is
for inspiration and entertainment only



*First published by AuthorHouse 3/6/2007*

*ISBN: 978-1-4343-0270-0 (sc)*

*Printed in the United States of America*
*Bloomington, Indiana*

*This book is printed on acid-free paper.*

# *Dedication & Acknowledgements*

*This book is dedicated to*
*the Celebrities herein*

Acknowledgements:

Gracious gratitude is expressed to all who assisted in the completion of this book so it could go out to the world for the highest good of all.

Cover, Artist & Layout: Mitch Harski
Editor: Rebecca Sullivan

Inspirational & Admin Support:

My mother, Jane
Dave, Ntathu, Sharon, MeLissa, Buz
Bob Korman: Backcover Photograph

***The Wisdom of the Stars Is Here to Ignite Your Personal & Global Dreams!***

## *Table of Contents*

# *Introduction*

*Connection with Celebrities in Spirit*

As I began my own prophetic and healing work, Elvis Presley was one of the first Celebrities to communicate with me clairaudiently (through inner hearing) and clairvoyantly (through inner seeing). Along the way, many other celebrities in spirit have come forth in communication with me, always confirming their presence and inspiring this book "when the time was right." Each chapter highlights my introductory connection with the celebrities through spirit communication.

*Celebrities in Spirit* reminds all that personal growth and positive thought should be a focus every day of life. The power keys and visualizations from the celebrities at the end of each chapter emphasize the importance of seeing the world in a multicultural, multi-denominational way.

This book features special messages of wisdom and insights for success in all arenas of life, from fifteen celebrities in spirit. These beautiful discourses from famous and respected beings from the realms "over the rainbow" are presented to uplift and inspire as you feel their presence. As you learn to open your heat and seek the highest truth and wisdom, you will be the beholder of great gifts indeed. For in the end, the greatest life success prevails through Higher Understanding. May *Celebrities in Spirit* inspire you in a magnificent transformation.

**Color Guide: Each Celebrity has a focus with one of 12 color rays: Blue** - Will & Faith; **Pink** - Love; **Yellow** - Creativity; **White Crystal** - Purification; **Green** - Healing & Truth; **Ruby** - Devotion; **Violet** - Freedom/Justice; **AquaMarine** - Clarity; **Coral/Peach** - Joy; **Gold** - Wisdom & Abundance; **Magenta** - Compassion; **Diamond Opal Essence** - All that Is.

**Celebrity Color Ray Chart is on page 112.**

# Chapter 1

## *Afterlife Wisdom of Princess Diana*

### *Connection with Princess Diana in Spirit*

What more does Princess Diana have to convey to the world today from the heavenly realms? Her legend lives on and she has a lot to say about humanity, her life's mission while in the body, and the continuance of her mission in Spirit. One can call upon her for assistance in life through her Power Key Focus for self-mastery, enlightenment and leadership.

Princess Diana first appeared to me on August 31, 1997, at the time of her passing, while I was on the island of Maui, Hawaii, receiving my ministerial ordination at the top of Mt. Haleakala. It was most profound, as I began praying for her and sending her into the Golden Light. She told me we were of the same soul family and that she would be with me throughout my path to create special projects.

I am most pleased to be in communion with her, and she often conveys special messages to others who have an affinity with her and her projects. Her keynote theme music is "Candle in the Wind" by Elton John (the version he sang at her funeral in 1997), which makes her presence most clear. I both see her and hear her in direct voice, which is a great honor; she usually appears in a magenta (compassion) robe with crown on her head. She connects me with others who have projects for children in support of her new educational system. Her contribution to humanity continues as she addresses education and assistance to deprived children, and one is greatly inspired through the radiance of her legacy of Compassion.

Those who are challenged along their path can surely find uplifting inspiration through "England's Rose," as her compassion and grace are alive in all our hearts as we open to the Rose within.

## Discourses from Princess Diana in Spirit - Self-Mastery and Leadership

**Q. What would you be doing now if your life on earth were extended?**

A. First of all, when I took my leave through the tunnel of Golden Light, I was lifted into the heavenly realms by thousands of angels of comfort, and I was shown the outpouring of millions of people in prayer. I am deeply grateful for all the love and prayers that have and still do greatly assist me here. I was deeply touched at how much my life had assisted others, for this is the greatest honor.

If I were still on Earth today, I would be doing extensive humanitarian work, speaking out in broadcasts and press interviews for world peace and justice, expressing my insights about global concerns for humanity's highest good, even in controversial matters (such as ending war, banning all landmines, and curtailing nuclear armament), in order to bring Truth to the masses. I would form charitable foundations to help humanity. I would be happily remarried and working closely with my children on their life endeavors. I would have my own television show to promote the healing of humanity and universal spiritual education for children.

I would work toward much higher objectives for the countries of the world that need the most assistance, and especially for the neglected and abused women and children of the world. I would create foundations to accomplish these goals and form a united group to address issues of poverty and deprivation on the planet. I would be working in world peace organizations to bring about peaceful resolutions and endorsing a Department of Peace for all other countries.

In the end, forgiveness and unconditional love reign. My role as Princess Diana allowed me the exposure I needed to fulfill my mission. I accomplished what I needed to and learned many difficult life lessons in that role. Most of all, I learned to fully love and respect myself, and I found the true purpose that fulfilled my life, in addition to raising my children, which was global humanitarian work.

**Q. How are you serving humanity from the higher realms?**
A. I work in the Celestial Legion of Compassion (Order of the Rose, Magenta Ray), which has an etheric retreat over Machu Picchu, Peru. The Divine Mother Mary oversees this Order and many other great beings belong, such as Mother Theresa. As a teacher in the realms of Compassion, I assist with subtle purification radiance to open humanity's hearts and minds to higher understanding, empowerment and enlightenment. The special focus of my work is to assist the celestial and earthly Indigo and Crystal Children in healing and teaching others to live in Truth, Love and Peace.

By my endeavors on Earth some of this work was started, and now it continues. Although my life on Earth seemed curtailed, I accomplished much and my mission on behalf of the Celestial Realm continues in radiant ways through the Magenta Crystalline Light, which purifies and lifts many souls who are seeking their true life path. In my role overseeing the higher spiritual education of children of all ages, I am creating alternative systems and programs. Another important focus of is to assist abused and abandoned children and purify humanity's negative patterns into positive. I also play a diplomatic role in assisting the world from these realms.

The establishment of the new higher educational system encompasses the full range of the arts and academic studies, along with holistic, spiritual and esoteric teachings, and wellness. This is important, as many evolved souls (star, crystal and indigo) are here and are much more advanced than their parents in terms of intuitive, spiritual, and creative gifts as well as evolved awareness. These children are calling out for advanced learning, as they are bored with the current systems.

Many advanced children are master souls that have come into the body to help lead the world to its new consciousness. To this aim, the hierarchy of light in the celestial realms is supporting a new educational system, which is already in the planning and projecting stages. The new system will be administered by a council that will oversee the broadest scope of teachings and programs by the best world teachers. This is a project of great magnitude that will be administered in many countries. I am pleased to hold a focus for this new educational system along with others. It will indeed be a grand and successful system and all those of affluence are encouraged to support this endeavor for the good of all. I thank you for your support and for following the call of your heart.

As another part of my service to humanity, I hold a diplomatic role in the celestial realms, as I had much experience of this while on Earth. Many who have played roles in the political arena while in the body on Earth also do so here. I serve as a Divine Order Diplomat along with many others in these realms, assisting those in global leadership roles through energy transmissions as guided by the Divine.

As a Divine Order Diplomat, I am able to intervene in many situations of a global nature in which I can send transcendent frequencies of light and soften the mindsets of those who have blinders on and whose hearts have hardened, so they can see the higher vision of global peace. In this way, densities and darkness on this planet can shift to light, harmony and peace. There is Free Will of course: all can choose the higher or lower roads, so to speak; but we open their consciousness to help them make decisions from a more enlightened perspective.

As Divine Order Diplomats, we also assist in political negotiations so resolutions can be made for the highest good, especially when there is much hostility and degeneration. For instance, when a summit meeting takes place, we from the etheric realms send a radiance of light to the participants, which is a thoughtform of sustaining peace and harmonious outcome. While it is more likely to be received by those who are open to the message, we are always monitoring these meetings.

Along with others in these realms, I hold a focus with global leaders and policy makers to help them govern from their hearts. Eventually everyone will learn this, as the consciousness on this planet is evolving into a more peaceful and harmonious one, governing with compassion, fairness and truth. Eventually everyone will learn that this is the only way to govern in accordance with the universal law of cause and effect (the principle also known as karma).

The more the world opens up to link with those in this realm, the more progress can be made for the greatest good of all. So we call to you to unite with us in this way to sustain the balance of vision and harmony of knowledge, and give assistance in areas of greatest need and crisis.

I again reaffirm that when all are sustaining the vision with us in these situations; great works are done; you are the ground team and we are the heaven team working with you. As we unite together with you, much more is accomplished and accelerated. It is important to be aware of Earth-plane world situations, as that awareness can transcend and bring the victories that are needed. Many have become complacent to world events, so my message is to be aware. Remember, you are in this world, but not of it; and as you link with us to transcend negativity and create a New Golden World, so it is done. I thank you in gracious gratitude from these realms for all your efforts.

**Q Now that you know what you know, what would you have done differently in your life?**

I would have loved more and spent more time with my children, as they are Crystal Children and the true leaders of the future. I would not have taken life so seriously and would have enjoyed more of my journey. I would have expanded my global humanitarian work and done even more to help those in need. I would have spoken out more for those who could not speak for themselves. I would have established a higher universal spiritual education system to advance the children. As I saw Mother Theresa as my role model, I would have spent more time with her listening to her wisdom.

I would have written the books I postponed writing, for our time on Earth is truly short. I speak from these realms to inspire all those who have a dream or special project they have not yet accomplished because of procrastination. Hold strong to your vision and go forward now with your life goals; acquire a mentor to help you and it will unfold. Call upon us in the Order of the Rose and you will receive unlimited Sacred Radiance to assist in your endeavors. All that is done to help humanity is rewarded in unlimited ways in accordance with universal law - giving and receiving, the other aspect of the karma concept.

I would have listened more to evolved teachers and sages, and focused more on my spiritual evolvement and self-mastery. I would have striven to be more present in the moment, attuned with the Divine. I began to see in my later years how all my experiences had come to play a part in the whole bigger picture for the world.

All in all, I accomplished and experienced a great deal in the short time I was on Earth, and the great outpouring of love and devotion at the time of my passing was a testament that I had made a difference. I lived the role that I played as Princess Diana in the best way I could. Now I am able to work more intimately with the masses in healing and transformation for higher purposes. When I am called upon, I assist others to open to their higher spiritual path so they may reach their true potential while in the body.

As it is, I have great influence from these realms in many world situations beyond human comprehension; in this way, along with many others I work to send forth thought forms and light frequencies to shift dense and dismal situations into lighter, more productive ones. My work continues in higher dimensions with the Order of the Rose. We have a great Agenda to carry out, and it brings me great joy to do so.

**Q. What do you see for the future of Planet Earth?**
A. Much has been done by millions of evolved souls and "lightworkers" on Earth to progress humanity. This has assisted us in the Celestial realms to transcend negative energies at a higher rate, thus bringing to light many earthly injustices. I also assist in Beloved St. Germain's Legion for Forgiveness, Transmutation, Freedom and Manifestation. I hold a focus for female empowerment and the Divine Feminine Energy.

The balance of Divine Feminine (Compassion, Cooperation and Creativity) and Divine Masculine (Spiritual Power, Action and Strength) Energies is now being integrated with the masses on this planet. There have been major shifts towards compassion through global tragedies, and many will witness even greater shifts with more compassion and global cooperation in the next few years, with global tragedies minimized. The dark shells and shadows remaining are dissolving through the Violet Flame of Forgiveness and are passing into the Golden Light of Enlightenment and Peace. Truth, Justice and

Rightness shall prevail for the whole.

By the year 2008, there will be a major planetary occurrence which will bring forth all government leaders on this planet to open up to the Divine Will of the Divine Creator and thus change their Agenda to that of Divine World Order, Compassionate Alliance, Preservation of the Environment, Wellness, and Abundance for all. Overall accelerated progression towards a Global Humanitarian Society will manifest, as this plan is already in effect now. Humanity will take back its true power from past disenfranchisements and Soul Enlightenment will prevail. Victory and Peace through compassion and understanding, united as one: this will set forth the New Golden Age on this planet and will oversee and implement the new structure for your world, the new template for this planet.

**Q. What guidance do you have for the empowerment of women as world leaders and teachers?**

A. First of all, I would advise women of all ages to always fulfill their heart and soul desires in both personal and career areas. Women are most certainly gifted in understanding others and are indeed gifted with talents as world leaders and teachers. They must teach men to be open to more compassionate leadership. The balance of the Divine Masculine and Feminine within all is important for true success. By this, I mean the creative, compassionate self balanced with the empowered, take-action self.

As the roles of women have changed, they will take their place in higher positions of world government in the near future, especially between 2005 and 2008. As a result of the higher dimensional consciousness on this planet, full respect and honor of women as well as men in leadership roles will be realized. My most direct guidance for young women is: Heal and Learn from the Past, Trust Yourself, Project the Highest Vision for Yourself and Humanity, and Go Forward with Absolute Confidence. Seek a Spiritual Advisor/Coach and call upon the Order of the Rose for assistance in clearing obstacles and raising your vibrations to succeed in your life's endeavors. One should realize that one is truly worthy of having it all: happiness, love, abundance and fulfillment of life's purpose.

**Q. What wisdom do you have for world leaders and dignitaries?**
A. There are universal laws that must be followed by all souls, and when there is interference, consequences always occur. From the standpoint of karmic law, no act escapes the consequences of other actions or repercussions. It is time for world leaders to take a more global humanitarian approach in their leadership, rather than acting out of power and greed. What "goes around" is "coming around" much more quickly and harshly than before. From these realms, we hold a focus for Divine Compassion wherever there is injustice, and millions of celestial beings work unendingly to transcend and redirect energies for the highest good of the planet. Much has been done and the major energy grid systems of the planet are now anchored in higher golden light to accomplish Divine Will on Earth.

In the end, all choices affect the whole and all Higher Truth is coming to the surface now; nothing goes unnoticed in the universal light, and it is time for this planet to come into the fullness of Light, Love and Balance. Actions taken for the Highest Good of All are thusly rewarded. We have no time for old authoritarian and self-serving acts that affect humanity adversely. In the next few years, we will feel a "turning." This has already begun as this planet rises into the 4th- and 5th- dimensional levels.

**Q. What message do you have for your sons?**
A. I walk beside them often. I am always there for important decisions. I send them my love with hugs and kisses. I take them on journeys in their dreams, and to connect more with me they can call to me before sleeping and I will help them remember the time we spent there. I will not interfere with their lessons, but still I will gently guide them.

I am so proud of them both and the stars shine brightly for their goals and dreams. They should not allow any interference to hold them back. They should hold strong to their visions and have no limits. Each has his special gifts and talents and will achieve beyond his dreams. I send a symbol of a shooting star and a double rainbow to each of them. They too have strong intuition and gifts of inner vision.

**Q. What advice, guidance, or message of inspiration do you have for the world?**

A. I send a wink and a smile to all, especially those in my homeland of England. Stand strong within yourselves. I send to each of your heart centers a full-blossomed Magenta Rose, that you may remember that you are the Rose of Life.

We are all a part of the wheel of life, playing out our part in the best way we know; hopefully learning and seeing the important things we need to learn and strengthening all the while who and what we are.

It is important to take time daily to reflect on what the lessons were for that day, what you have gained and what you have given, as well as what you have accomplished overall. Let the waterfalls clear away the rest and lift your spirits to the more important values and symbols of life. You cannot find true sense of purpose or happiness from others around you, not even in the work you do or the goals you set. You can only find a true sense of contentment inside from knowing who you are, seeing the role you play in this life and your higher purpose, and keeping the vision of the highest and best for your life and that of others. Do not hold on to past regrets or beliefs that no longer serve.

So I advise you to unburden yourself and be the Prince or Princess inside yourself first and foremost. You are a special being playing out a special role in this body, and life passes quickly. Take more time for play and joy in life; the rest will take care of itself. As you detach from the mundane trivialities of the world, you will see what is truly important; it is then that all will flow in synchronicity. When the challenges show themselves, welcome them with a smile as if to say, "Now I can rise above this and gain strength; this too shall pass and it is for the Highest Good."

I would like to convey that attunement with a higher power, whatever your spiritual path, is most important. When people are praying, meditating and focusing on higher attunement, we in these realms are able to ignite through them like a power generator and expand the frequencies of prayer and meditation. We in these realms are constantly sending light to all; it is indeed like a volcanic explosion filled with sparks of light. When one prays or meditates, one attunes to this higher source (like plugging into a grand light socket), and we are able to link with humanity.

We from these realms applaud all those who come together; when two or more are gathered, great miracles take place. The more people focus on peace within themselves and the world, the more this accelerates shifts within themselves and the world. If the entire world were to join in synchronicity with a global project twenty-four hours a day, seven days a week, much more would be done for the progress of this planet. If one held a single point of focus on peace and harmony even for a minute each day, the full scope of progress that would be made would be unimaginable.

I speak on the subject of coming into the knowing, and having absolute confidence. We speak to those souls who do not fully believe that their prayers and meditations make a difference or are being honored. It is with higher vibrations of clear intent in prayer, mediation, affirmation, and projection with absolute confidence, that miracles take place instantly.

Absolute confidence and knowing within oneself makes a difference in manifesting that, which is the highest good for all. When one has absolute confidence in knowing, all is accomplished: no doubts, fears or illusions remain, the dichotomy is transcended, and only true light compassion is left.

Many are at different levels. It matters not how prayers are said, nor who is praying: only the heartfelt focus of prayer matters. All prayers and meditations done through monasteries, churches, temples and other places of prayer contribute a great service to the world.

### Princess Diana's Power Key of Self-Mastery & Leadership

The 3-Minute Tune-Up is easy to apply in one's daily routine. It is recommended that the 3-Minute Tune-Up and Rose Visualization be practiced three times daily if possible (in the morning, at noon, and in the evening), or at least once daily at noon to synchronize with as many others as possible. This is important; it is in this moment of alignment that one hears with the heart, and in this way, all things are possible. It is our hope in these realms that you memorize and use this valuable practice, in addition to any other practices you already have as a daily routine, so that you will witness the effects in your life.

May this practice bring to you the Grace from which it has come.

PRINCESS DIANA'S 3-MINUTE TUNE-UP (the 3 R's)

RELEASE all fear, doubt, and negativity while invoking and breathing in the Blue-Violet Flame of Forgiveness to flow through your head, throat, heart, solar plexus, and abdomen into the center of the earth. *Focus for 1 minute, while taking 12 deep breaths,* ***"I forgive, release and set myself and all free now."***

REALIGN yourself through Divine compassion, invoking and breathing in the Magenta Flame to flow through every cell and level of your being. *Focus for 1 minute, taking 12 deep breaths,* ***"I realign with full clarity and balance now."***

RECREATE a focused Vision for yourself and the world by invoking the Golden Flame of infinite possibilities to flow into every cell at every level and dimension of your being. See the highest visions for yourself and the world. Focus for 1 minute, taking 12 deep breaths, **"I recreate victoriously for the highest good of all."** (cross hands over heart in Gratitude)

Princess Diana's Rose Visualization

Envision the heart and mind of the Divine Mother Earth as one with your heart. Integrate this magnificent Heart Focus within every thought, word and action in your life. Let Heartfelt Kindness and Compassion be your focus. Meditate on millions of radiant crystalline Magenta Flame rose petals floating from the celestials, saturating and purifying every cell of humanity. Visualize all consciousness opening to greatest Compassion, Empowerment and Cooperation. Affirm gratitude at the end of all visualizations.

AFFIRMATION: I AM ONE WITH SELF-MASTERY & SUCCESS

*In Loving Compassion to All,*
*Princess Diana*

# Chapter 2

## *Afterlife Wisdom of Elvis Presley*

### *Connection with Elvis Presley in Spirit*

Yes, Elvis is alive and with us in spirit! Through the following powerful communications he reveals how he is assisting the world, especially musicians and artists, by higher inspiration from the celestial realms. In his communication, he shares with us the depth of symbolism in many of the songs he performed while he was on Earth. It is hoped that you will feel his magical presence through these messages and be even more inspired by his wonderful music, wisdom and charm, which live on forever. He most often appears to me in cobalt blue suits or robes, which symbolizes Will, Communications, Faith and Personal Power.

To my surprise, Elvis Presley was one of the first spiritual beings that I received direct voice messages and visions from. Whilst deeply honored, I did not understand his connection with me as a messenger for others. He later confirmed to me that we spent several lifetimes together, once in Polynesia where we were royalty, sang together and were very close.

On the island of Kauai, Elvis Presley relayed some messages to me that I passed on to the musician Larry Rivera. At the time, I did not understand why I had to pass on this message. I did not know this, but during the filming of Blue Hawaii at Coco Palms, Larry and Elvis became close friends. When Larry heard the message, tears came to his eyes. He understood the message as meant for him.

To me this was evidence and confirmation that this being was indeed Elvis, communicating messages to me through my inner hearing. In time, as I came to know and trust Elvis's presence, I received other messages, which I passed on. Each message was confirmed and understood by its receiver.

Elvis Presley would flash in at times when I was most discouraged on my path. On one occasion, he even had dinner with me in his essence when I needed help most. This was a comfort and a great blessing. Elvis's special song "The Wonder of You" would play at times when he was trying to communicate messages for me or for others. I now hear Elvis with crystal clarity. I have come to know him as the great being and healer he is, especially in the field of music and the arts, and to those who have lost their path through life's challenges.

**Discourses from Elvis Presley in Spirit - Achieving True Dreams**

**Q. What was your mission on Earth and now in spirit?**

A. I see now that my mission was to help heal humanity's hearts through music. Music is a very powerful ministry, depending on the levels one wishes to take it. Many of my songs had hidden symbolism, which I will go into a little here; many of the lyrics help people at deeper levels, bringing happiness and enthusiasm to all. I saw that many people need this, and still do. From these realms, my musical ministry lives on. I work with the Blue Light Ray and the Golden Light. Through these Lights, I often inspire musicians and artists in a higher vibration. I can help people more closely when they are playing my music. This is the link I have with them. Therefore, you see, not only am I still alive, I am very much continuing my musical legend from these dimensions. There is a lot of work to be done to help humanity. Let me tell you, it is non-stop here!

Often we play out situations kind of like the TV Show Touched by an Angel. We do not always appear in physical form, but we come in our spiritual bodies to inspire and encourage people on their life paths. I also see my mission here as helping others to create through inspirational music that we send in a form called "music of the spheres." I also hold a focus to help people who have lost their way, whether emotionally or through addictions.

I help these people to open their hearts again, to see who they really are, what their purpose or mission is in the earthly body, and to know there is a rainbow just around the corner. The music is really in your heart and everyone has music to play in one way or another. So I come today to inspire all of you to let that music play, and discover your true purpose and talents in this lifetime, for it really is short. A lifetime in the body flashes by very quickly, so why not open up to all its possibilities and let your heart sing?

What I did was no greater than what any of you can do in your lives; whether you are famous or not does not matter. It is not how much money you have, but who you are that matters in life. When you are true to yourself, others will be true to you also.

So my mission continues here in the Blue Light, which is Faith, Communication, Will, Power and Courage, and I come today to inspire you in this way. To go forward in your own personal power and courage in life is a great step, and the universe will respond to you. No matter how many obstacles come along, just smile at them and know that dreams do come true. The delays are all part of the big plan; don't try to figure it out, but just let it flow along, holding on to a higher vision for yourself and others. Don't get caught up in the little stuff; it's not important in the end. When you leave this life, you are shown on a screen what you have accomplished, what you could have accomplished, and what your true mission was. Then you know if you did the best you could.

Another important part of my mission here is to help others overcome and transcend addictions to reach their full potential. As a healer of hearts, I work in these realms to uplift and assist those who are discouraged, lonely or lost. I do this through my music and through the Blue Light, which I work with among many other celestial beings.

Most of us know what it is like to feel lonely and sad and I felt this at times as I was isolated from normal society. I missed the normal "country boy" kind of life I had when I was younger. My music helped me through my times of sadness when my mother passed over and after my marriage ended. Addictions, whether medications, food, alcohol, drugs, or material things, serve nothing except as a bandage. The key to overcoming all challenges is to recognize, believe and value yourself enough. The Blue Light, inner contemplation and invocation of Higher Will leads to victory over all challenges.

**Q. What inspiration would you like to give humanity about your music?**

A. I would like to go into the symbolism of some of my music as it relates to humanity. Much of my musical inspiration still gets through to musicians today if they tune in to me. I can help them to open to higher creativity and success.

**"Love Me Tender" (My signature tune)**

Love in this song should not be seen only in a romantic sense, but as a higher universal Love. Many of my songs extend into a higher presence or consciousness. The key here is creating and manifesting through the Blue Light. The expression from "out of the blue" means everything is created from the ether, a higher source. This vibration creates a natural, blissful "high," and the need for a superficial high through drug use dissolves. When you vibrate with a higher natural energy, you hold the Key to obtaining the peace within. *Love me Tender* brings out the higher electric energy. I was tapping into a Blue Light Energy force field, which ignites and brings in Truth, Power, Will, Faith, Protection, and Communication with the Higher Power. The peace of reconnection with the soul comes forth through it. The tender Love of the universal light is what we are seeing, and it is through compassion that we all find it with one another. Remember to be true to yourself in a tender, loving way, and treat others as you would want them to treat you: it's a full circle.

**"Can't Help Falling in Love"**

This song also brings in the energy of universal Love through the Heart. "Like a river flows" is a reference to the spiritual flow within. Open the waters to let them flow through the heart. Your level of openness determines how much you receive of Electric Blue Energy, Divine creativity and healing of heart and soul. As I work in the Order of the Blue Lotus (soul enlightenment), my music goes on through the Blue Light of Higher Will (power, strength, courage and faith). Many of my songs bring this energy through, many felt this energy when I played in live concerts and were in awe of it. The electric power of the Blue Light flowed through, ignited their souls, and inspired them.

### "Teddy Bear"

The Teddy Bear symbolizes gentleness with self and with others. It calls people to become one with each other, with nature and Mother Earth. In addition, it implies forgiveness for one another, being kind and living in harmony. We all know Teddy Bears open up the heart, which was the intention of this song.

### "Don't Be Cruel"

This song is a reminder to treat others with compassion and tenderness, as you yourself wish to be treated. It also has a deeper meaning, to go within the Self to see what inner barriers may be holding you back from opening to a fulfilling relationship. Often people have swept a lot of pain and repressed feelings aside, and this blocks them from knowing what their heart is telling them. It's easy to put "bandages" on the old wounds, but it's better to heal them in the end. If I had done this, my life would have surely been extended. Remember to seek counseling from spiritual advisers and healers to help dissolve the past more easily. Do not let your anger affect others who care about you. You can rise above it all and be true to your own heart.

### "Blue Suede Shoes"

This song symbolically represents refusal to let anyone take one's power away. I did this when I let others control my work and creativity instead of overseeing all matters personally. "Blue Suede Shoes" is a direct reminder to people to stand up for their empowerment in a higher way and not allow others to treat them like doormats. Self-love and self-worth increases when one stands strong in one's personal power.

### "The Wonder of You"

This is a special keynote song to let Athena know when I am around.

When on Earth, I was misunderstood, as are many artists. I got caught up in the limelight and lost touch with reality, with myself. When others appear to hurt us along the way, this song can lift us out of the sadness. It is intended to unlock a doorway to one's self. It is about the Real You. Lines like "You are always there to lend a hand in everything I do" and "You give me strength to carry on" refer to the higher power.

**"Hound Dog"**

The lines, "You ain't nothing but a hound dog/Crying all the time," mean not to let emotions get the better of you in life. My message is to change old patterns of depression or regrets about the past to higher, positive ones. If you refuse to dwell on the sorrows of the past a shift can take place; you will find a light way of lifting yourself out of the doldrums. This can be shifted in vibration and many spiritual advisers, healers and consultants can assist with these shifts. Nothing is ever resolved by staying in the lower vibration of sadness or regret. As you learn, seek, and ask for help, angels and friends come along to help you to into the new levels. When you ask, you open to unlimited possibilities in your life. When you stay in the lower vibrations of remorse and sadness, you spiral downward. In those levels you block yourself, like a two-door Chevy spinning in the mud. You cannot hold regrets or harbor revenge against others as it only hurts you in the end, so move on beyond it.

Gospel music helped me to heal myself and others. Recording the album *How Great Thou Art* was a success because those songs mattered to me. This was an important period in my life for me, and I would have liked to continue with all kinds of spiritual music concerts and tours. Unfortunately, I allowed the business to influence me and later started to lose my focus for my spiritual path.

All my music was meant to uplift and cheer people. When I lost myself along the way and the haze set in, I did not create new music. It was my joy on Earth to work on songs and productions that made a difference, so now I do it through the Etheric realms, and I work through many musicians, especially when they call upon me. The music is in the Etheric, the music of the spheres.

**Q. Knowing what you know now, what would you be doing had your life been extended?**

A. I would certainly have taken better care of myself spiritually, mentally, emotionally and physically. I would have sought out the best teachers and healers to help me stay focused on a universal path of Higher Truth. (The book Elvis by the Presleys references my quest for Truth in the chapter "The Seeker.") I would have performed more universally spiritual music and done more such concerts. I loved the movies and would have liked to do more, but then the Earth is a stage and there are plenty of movies to go around. It is all in the role you play, so play it as well as you can; you make the choices.

In addition, I would be involved in more humanitarian foundations and projects for the world, raising funds to help humanity and influence politics. I would have been more politically involved to make the world a better place, and would have used my prominence in the media in order to accomplish this.

I would have established a special musicians' foundation for funding and supporting exceptionally talented artists and musicians (especially those who could not afford tuition at regular schools).. They in turn would help fund others through the same program later on. I would have liked to create another "Renaissance" of artists and musicians, to help heal the world faster through creative expression.

On a personal note, I would have made my family and loved ones a major priority, healed the wounds of the past, and taken more time to "hear the music." I would have had a more fulfilling personal life filled with happiness with my loved ones and close friends. I would have loved more tenderly and with more compassion for others.

Pure Love is the greatest power in the world and with it, all is possible.

After a while one learns the greatest gift is service and devotion to humanity. This is what I do here in these realms with many others in the Order of the Blue Lotus (including Himalayan Masters such as Yogananda) for humanity's enlightenment. I wish to extend gracious gratitude to all who have prayed and lit candles for me for so long. This has helped me in my own evolvement and thus has helped open the hearts of humanity in a greater way.

**Q. What messages do you have for your loved ones on Earth?**

A. For Lisa Marie, I would first like to say you are in my heart of hearts. You have come through many life lessons and have risen above them all with flying colors! I have been with you, to inspire you and encourage you, both in dream state and in the conscious thoughts I send forth to you and the family. I am so proud of you and watch over you and your family with tender loving care. I also want to acknowledge in gratitude the wonderful book recently published in my honor by Priscilla and you. It was a great lift in my heart to see so many read it and be uplifted by it, because it speaks the truth, and presents a clear picture of who I was. It has opened many hearts, and we are together forever. I love you both and thank you very much. I surround you both with the Blue Crystal Light of Protection and will always watch over the entire family through this life and beyond. I am sending Lisa Marie a special blue crystalline gem Stone that will come to her soon, from my heart directly to hers. It will be given to her in a very special way, so that she will know it is from me. It will help her in her music, communication, and faith. I send it to her in thought-form, and it will manifest in physical form as a symbol of my presence with her. I am working with her from these levels so she will feel and know my presence. Like my loved ones who have already passed on, I continue to be a guardian for others on Earth.

I am glad Lisa Marie is following her dreams. She is a shining star, very bright. She will be very successful in music, and an example to inspire and empower other women. She has great compassion for others, as does her mother.

I send my unending, unconditional love to both Lisa Marie and Priscilla. They will always be in my heart of hearts. For them I send "Love Me Tender" as a symbol of my endless love and gratitude.

**Q. What advice/inspiration do you have for musicians and artists?**

A. To be a great musician is to perform from the heart; let it flow through the heart to others, not the mind. Also, give back to society what it has given to you.

Call upon us here and we will send high vibrations of light rays to assist in the fields of art and music.

Remember, in life you can't take anything with you. You can make a difference in your life's role and purpose, and to find that is the greatest gift. My advice to those who have so many talents and gifts is to follow the vision, and when you feel you are discouraged, call upon us here; learn to meditate and change your thought process to envision what you really want and it will happen.

The symbolism of my music stood for faith and love within. My way of giving back is to inspire and direct positive energies to those who are lost in the shuffle, to guide, help and inspire them. Sometimes we send other people such as friends and family to help along the path. I have assisted many musicians and artists on the Earth plane and I am here for whoever calls on me, for there are no limits in these realms.

I send illumination to all musicians, artists, and those who call, for igniting of their soul's purposes will break open the doorways for the highest dreams and happiness. The spiritual path is the most important thing you can do to fulfill your purpose; there are many paths, but choose one that is without barriers or controls so you are free to excel to higher vibrations and attune with the Higher Power.

Instead of pursuing the opportunities that offer more money, remember it is far more rewarding to fulfill the dreams that make your heart sing. Meditation and contemplation on your visions is important. Always keep music and art as a hobby, even if they cannot be your main career: for when the door opens, you will be ready.

Being famous or wealthy is not the key to success. The greater joy and fulfillment has to come from deep inside of you. Open your heart and see that there are many avenues to fulfill your goals and dreams, whether it is a masterpiece in writing, art, music, or any other career endeavor.

Knock and the door will surely open, as that great One said 2000 years ago. You must face and release emotional baggage; get the assistance you need, practice self-contemplation, set your goals, and know the help is always there. Do not let peers and others influence you to self-destructive or addictive behavior. Call on us here and many angels will be there to assist you. Few there are who actually remember to ask for help or express gratitude when that help comes. According to the universal law of karmic return, the mistakes you make in this lifetime will be either repeated or corrected in the next, so why not get it right now?

Do not put your life on a back burner. Let the Electric Blue Lightning frequencies move you into the new.. Write your goals weekly and monthly and this will bring them sooner into physical reality. You do not need to figure them out in detail; they will happen when you are committed to the results.

Through my music I am able to “link in” more directly with others and lift their spirits, so they will not become discouraged with all the changes taking place on Earth now, and instead have hope and inspiration in knowing all is happening for the highest good. My music continues on through others’ music, when I send inspirational compositions and lyrics through to those who can receive them. Many beings here do this for those who will listen and receive. This is most easily done through meditation and “tuning in” each day.

When I was a young boy I had a vision of being a world-famous rock and roll star, and I knew in my soul it would happen, and my parents supported me. I knew in my heart and soul it was a part of me and I held on to the vision. I never gave up, even after the first Grand Ole Opry performance when the world was not quite ready for me. Then one day the floodgate opened and the rock and rolling started. There was a lot of judgment about my movements in performances, but it was all part of the play for more popularity....and it was great exercise! (Laughs) I had the gifts and talents, but I also had my faith and my visions, and I laid the foundation I needed to follow through within myself. My goals were to make people happy through music, make my parents proud, and help my mama. She is here with me and we are soulmates.

**Q. What is your special message to the world?**

A. Let Rock and Roll to create a bright new world for all through a deeper heart’s connection with the self and with others, and open to the highest creative potential and harmony for the planet. Sing your heart song. Dance your life dance. Be the artist you are supposed to be. Become the best you can be in your life and career. Follow that shining star and you will become who you truly are. Call on us from these realms and we will be there to assist. Let your own starlight shine brightly for the world to see.

**Elvis Presley’s Power Key: Achieving your true Dreams**

**BELIEVE**

*Believe in yourself and your dreams will come true*
*Envision your dreams already fulfilled; review your written list*
*Let Go* of fear thru daily use of the Blue Flame Visualization
*Ignite* your true confidence thru daily Affirmations.
*Establish* a success support team with Visionaries & Mentors
*Visualize* yourself with victorious results even when obstacles arise
*Embrace* all that comes to you in gracious gratitude to all

**Elvis Presley's Daily Blue Flame Visualization**

Invoke, visualize and breathe in the Cobalt BlueFlame Crystalline Waterfall of light above you in the name of the Order of the Blue Lotus (Himalayan Masters). Breathe in for 7 counts, hold 7 counts, and release 7 counts continuously throughout this 10-minute visualization.

Begin to envision thousands of bright blue stars and lotuses streaming down into the top of your head, filling every cell in your body. Feel the blue stars and lotuses clearing away all fear, doubt and negative emotions from every part of your being as they move through the head, throat, heart, solar plexus, abdomen, and down though your legs into the Earth. Begin to visualize the Creation you are working on, whether it is personal or career-oriented, bring the visualization into your heart center, and keep breathing into Oneness. Invoke gratitude and affirm "It is done."

Cross your hands over your heart to seal the energy and keep it sacred to yourself. Do this daily and you will have greater and faster results.

AFFIRMATION: I AM TOTAL FAITH IN ACHIEVING MY DREAMS

*All my Love tenderly,*
*Elvis*

# Chapter 3

## *Afterlife Wisdom of Judy Garland*

### *Connection with Judy Garland in Spirit*

Judy Garland "flashes" in when her movies are on or rainbows are present. Judy reminds me how important it is to follow your dreams, attuning to a deeper sense of self-worth to achieve the highest. Judy and others in the rainbow light help to shift the past and heal hearts to open to greater gifts. They enhance courage, strength and confidence. The vision of "tapping the red shoes three times" is inspiration to know that solutions and creations are all within the heart, the "home." Judy always appears in a white crystalline (Purification) and ruby (devotional power) gown, surrounded in rainbows with a crown on her head. Her keynote music is, of course, "Somewhere over the Rainbow." It is a pleasure to present her discourses.

Discourses from Judy Garland in Spirit - A Rainbow Life

Q. What was your mission on earth and in afterlife?
A. My role while on earth was to inspire the imagination of the world through music and theater. My most famous movie, *The Wizard of Oz*, was undoubtedly the greatest inspiration to the world about returning to the important qualities of life - attuning to the heart, mind and courage to see true purpose within the self. *The Wizard of Oz* also depicts the triumph of Light over darkness, an important part of my message to the world.

I work in the Legions of the Rainbow Light here in the celestial realms. We help uplift souls into happiness so they can more easily attain their missions while on earth. Many people have lost the enthusiasm and the confidence to attain their dreams; we focus energies and thoughtforms to assist them in breaking through barriers, so they can achieve a rainbow life.

All fairytales are divinely inspired. "Somewhere over the Rainbow" implies that dreams do come true. *The Wizard of Oz* had a great deal of higher symbolism for the world. In the movie, we discover that everything comes from our inner resources; personal strengths attain the greatest success. In the words of Dorothy, "If I ever go looking for my heart's desire again, I won't look any farther than my own backyard." Home is where the heart is, and within the heart is all inspiration.

**Q. What would you have done differently, now that you know what you know?**

A. In the rainbow light I still play the role of Dorothy, finding and helping others find their truth and courage within. I would have accomplished more on earth if I had been more enlightened about my soul mission then. I would have been able to see that earth life was one level, but not the higher reality. Over the rainbow all things are possible.

I would have pursued deeper personal growth and healing of issues so I could have been a more effective role model for others. *The Wizard of Oz* is great teaching for the masses. I am very pleased I am able to inspire so many for so long; I would have tried even harder to help others realize there is truly "no place like home" within the Self.

**Q. What message do you have for the world?**

A. I would like to remind adults and children who are depressed, or stressed from experiences of catastrophes or traumas, that they are never alone. To those affected by abandonment or neglect, realize this trauma can be overcome and "somewhere over the rainbow" miracles can happen. Call upon your angels and they are there to assist from the celestial realms. It is important to be strong within the self; build your inner house well and it will shelter you.

Through the rainbow of rays we bring forth today, we wish to tell you to take time to play as a child would. Take time for that which brings faith and joy, for this will bring fulfillment. Like the characters in *The Wizard of Oz*, you, too, will find all you need within yourself. And so I come to remind you, dear ones, that you have everything already within you to shift situations, to change and create. The "pot of gold" you seek outwardly will never be found, for the true gold is within your heart.

**Q. What is your inspiration for women?**
A. "Click your heels three times and make a wish." My most important message is to look to the inner beauty. In my role as Judy Garland, I did not take care of my health and often abused my body through addictions to maintain the "perfect body" for the film industry; so I've learned that wellness on all levels should always be the priority in one's life. Addictions are merely the bandage for deeper issues, which easily dissolve through holistic assistance.

I could not feel the inner pain and it all erupted within me, but all I needed was the right assistance to help shift my energy to command what I needed for my body and my soul. It is not easy to be always in the limelight; the long hours and demands for perfection were so great. This is more balanced now, as there is greater respect for women in the industry.

I commend women who continue to stand up for their rights and for the equality they deserve in career life. Do not be affected by outer judgments from society. Empower your life with self-nurturing and a focus on total wellness. Do not allow others to control you or diminish your own personal power in any way. You are in charge of your destiny; recognize incongruent situations that affect your wellness, being or focus. Make decisions in dignity and courage, creating the doors that will open to your new rainbows.

### Judy Garland's Power Key to a Rainbow Life

RAINBOW
Remember to follow your dreams
Activate the gifts within yourself
Improve your innate talents and skills
Never lose confidence in yourself
Believe in your worthiness to have it all
Open to self-development and enlightenment
Within you is the fulfillment of a Rainbow Life

### Judy Garland's Rainbow Visualization

Visualize a beautiful ruby flame, a pillar of liquid crystalline light above you as it pours through all of your being. Breathe in for 7 counts, hold 7 counts and release 7 counts throughout the 10-minute visualization. Continue as you are totally saturated in the ruby flame light beaming through you into the center of the earth. Focus on your heart center. Envision a triple rainbow extending out to a situation you want to create. See the rainbow linking in with your vision and activating it. Envision it all complete. Send out rainbows of light to all loved ones, friends, your community, and the world. See the entire Earth wrapped in multi-colored rainbows bringing new hope and inspiration to all of humanity. Click your heels three times. Voila! It is done!

AFFIRMATION: I NOW CREATE A RAINBOW LIFE OF SUCCESS

*Endless Rainbow Miracles to You!*
*Judy Garland (Crystalia)*

# Chapter 4

## *Afterlife Wisdom of Johnny Carson*

### *Connection with Johnny Carson*

Johnny Carson has been communicating with me and making me laugh since his passing over. He is really a master teacher. He always appears in a yellow/gold suit, sitting at a golden desk (a symbol of creativity and the arts). He has shown me evidence and conveyed messages to others who knew it was indeed his presence. He has much to say about the Show, which still goes on, he says, forever.

Several months after his passing over, I had a dream in which we were having dinner in a tall building overlooking the nightlights of NYC. He was telling me exactly why his show was such a success and how it really uplifted people, which was his primary intent. He is a great inspiration for this book and my work in the media. Again, it is an honor to present his magnificent discourses. Here's Johnny ...

Discourses from Johnny Carson in Spirit - Career Success

Q. What is your mission in the afterlife?
A. In the Legions of Creativity and the Arts, I help many with creativity in all aspects of life, especially the arts and music. I am a "grand choreographer" in the celestial realms, helping with many projects in film, TV, the arts and music that uplift and inspire through humor.

I work in these realms as a teacher and my service continues through the theater, art and film guilds here in the etheric; the show goes on! I help many upcoming artists and musicians, especially when they call on me to help them move through obstacles to their real purpose on earth. People need to lighten up; there is too much seriousness going on! It is time to clear out the old and bring in the new era, the Golden Age of Enlightenment.

In these realms, format does not matter; my role is to lighten the hearts and souls of others in every way possible, which is what I tried to do through The Tonight Show. \

**Q. What do you know now that you did not know on earth?**

A. How great it is here! At the point when I crossed over, I was shown on a screen all I had done right and wrong in that life. It was kind of like seeing your whole life on "reruns." The proof is always in the pudding, as the saying goes.

I was pleased to see that I was honored by all the many people on earth who sent love and prayers in gratitude for what I did on behalf of others. I was just doing my job the best way I knew and I never let go of my visions for success. It was my privilege to escort many through the celebrity doorways to inspire the world. Mostly I had a great time and I saw beyond the level of the physical body when I crossed over. I was lifted into the higher dimensions immediately and for this I was grateful.

I had my shortcomings, but overall I see clearly now why I was doing what I did - to inspire humanity through my gifts. I did work very hard and was a perfectionist; I would have changed that part and not been so critical of others and myself. Life is too short; it is a flash from the viewpoint in the afterlife.

I always envisioned the shows ahead of time and the ideas often came to me through flashes of inspiration from my guardian angels. We all have them, you know, so it's better to learn to communicate with other dimensions where the angels have a lot of help to give. I am now learning to be of greater service as a teacher through thoughtform, light, sound and color; we assist in raising vibrations wherever we can to attain greater creativity, enlightenment and peace on earth.

**Q. What is your message for the world about career and life success?**

A. (Vision: Johnny appeared in his golden suit with a golden turban on his head for this question) It matters not whether one is famous or not; career success has to do with your passion in life. Always trust in yourself and let the negative thoughts that come toward you roll off like water. Remember that humor is a gift and to be able to laugh at yourself is a greater gift. When you do this, everyone else around you can lighten up too.

The world needs more cosmic comedians who can wake humanity up through humor. It is important to remember the importance of humor, especially in the tense global situations. Levity and lightness are as contagious as fear and negativity. This is what I tried to do in the Tonight Show and it helped a lot of people, as do other talk shows. My success came through a lot of hard work, diligence and holding to my vision. I became the observer just playing my part and not so caught up in it all.

Children and adults like to feel that they are contributing to life. I know from these realms that everyone wants to feel important to society, to know that they are needed and serve a purpose. I remind all, especially the children, to get in touch with their true purpose on earth. What are your real inner talents? Do not focus on what you are not as good at, just because it brings money. Inner reflection, focus on your gifts and diligence, will bring you to your true career path. In addition, when you help others see their full potential, you open a secret doorway for them. I enjoyed seeing the contributions that others made to the world through their creativity. Even though they were not well known then, they were brought through the "doorway," and in this way all of us won; they brightened up the show, which brightened the world.

Even the Angels have a sense of humor. Humor takes a person out of the illusion that any particular situation has power over him or her. Think, for example, the next time you are overwhelmed or discouraged, of the golden laughing Buddha and bring him into your heart; this will lift you in moments of despair and bring your mind to humor and joy. This is a form of enlightenment, too, the ability to shift yourself out of negative into positive thought within an instant.

We all know that humor also uplifts in the political arena; humor dispels intensity and helps to balance and neutralize for a shift to a win-win outcome. Anger, hatred, terror, and fear create gridlock.

Humor, lightness, understanding, and positive thinking open the creative flow for solutions that unlock this.

I would like to inspire the global media circuit to host more inspirational and humorous shows to lighten and assist humanity rather than dwell on the negative. If we project positive thoughts for all catastrophic occurrences, humanity will move forward to greater awareness of unity. Humanity can surely use more humor and smiles of caring at this time of trouble, while the media magnifies doom and gloom. For as it has been said before, what you think, you create, and thought is contagious, my friends. A smile is worth a million words, so let the world smile with you. In fact, why not promote a "humor-contagious society," to offset the fear-contagious one?

Why not set a time at 12 noon everyday, when everyone around the world smiles at the person next to him or her and sends a positive thought or phrase? This sounds too simple; however, just doing this would make a big difference in the world. If everyone around the world sent the vision of a yellow smiling happy face to each other and the world at exactly high noon each day, there would be an incredible instantaneous shift for the planet. Humor and smiles are free - no cost, no burden, simply from the heart. Try it and I will join with you! "Happy faces around the world" would bring light to all shadows and have the effect of a global light bulb going on and staying on. It would transform the world into a humanitarian focus. Now, see the entire planet as a giant golden Happy Face and watch the world change!

Remember, there is truly no time and space and all can change instantaneously; as you think it, so it will be. It takes only a moment to create a miracle. In one moment, a new opportunity happens and you can become a millionaire; in another moment, a baby is born; a new project manifests to change the world. One can become a superstar in a moment, justice can be served in a moment, and choices can be made to help those in need. In one instant, the whole world could create peace among all; and nations could come together for the highest good when they "see" that self-serving decisions serve no one in the end. In an instant, mountains can move; through focus, we can balance out the economy, we can create jobs and make the choice to clean up the pollution on the planet. In an instant, humanity can take back its power to work together and demand true justice and integrity in world leadership.

I see from these realms there are already incredible projects and plans underway to heal this planet. One moment in time comes when all can be all that they can be, indeed. When group energy and group mind come together, it is like a huge volcano and no one can stop it. Let the volcano of unlimited possibilities erupt within your heart and in the world for the grand renaissance

Mountains are certainly going to be moving in a big way very soon. The world is calling for this and it is time. Group mind decides its destiny and think tanks create the plan and strategy for this to happen. It is fascinating from these realms to see this wonderful plan now activated for the earth. No one can interfere with this plan; it is a Done Deal! It is now being "downloaded" on the earth plane, so to speak. John Lennon, who is here, reveals that the song "Imagine" which came through to him from the etheric when he was in body is indeed a very powerful message. Affirm the full emphasis of that song with the earth as a golden happy face; even once a day at high noon, just imagine the great momentum of this energy to move mountains. Your thoughts are your golden key to accessing life's endless possibilities.

When all align with higher vibrations of positive thought and laughter, enthusiasm and joy, then the "real show" will begin! Limits are only in the mind that has not yet seen the full spectrum of creation. All is energy and all has a contagious effect so choose the "planetary happy face" and help shift the world. See for others what you wish for yourself. You came with the complete creation toolkit for total life success.

There are many in these realms who would love to be in closer communication with people on earth. Many people still have their mental/ emotional helmets on which block our direct communion with them. Therefore, I am here to help remove the helmets and break through the barriers. Remember, "You are a spiritual being having a human experience," in the words of Dr. Wayne Dyer. Listen and in the silent stillness of consciousness, you will hear us. In this way we can be of greater assistance at this most crucial time on earth. We communicate with you in light, sound, color and thoughtform; affirm each day that you can hear, see and know more in attunement with the celestial realms, and so it shall be. Advisors and teachers can, of course, accelerate the process. Remember, "People who need people are the luckiest people in the world." Sweep the past away (there are many sources to assist you in energetically cleansing the past) and move beyond to the new creations life has to offer you.

**Q. How would you have lived your life differently, now that you know what you know?**

A. Well, unbelievably, I would have laughed more! Because I was so busy creating humor for others, I could not see the humor for myself! Also, I would have taken better care of my health. I would have done more inner contemplation and pursued a deeper spiritual path of meditation. For the most part, I fulfilled not only my life purpose but also helped many along the way. I knew innately that generosity always returned to the giver.

**Q. What messages do you have for friends or loved ones?**

A. I send my best to Ed McMann. I sometimes visit Ed (and others) in dream state and we have good times and talks. I am very proud of him and the wonderful book he created portraying my life. He is my brother in spirit and I am very much with him and his family. There are "great shows" where I am also and we all work together to create "great shows" here in these realms. There are theater, actors, musicians, artists guilds here just like on earth. It is wonderful to be a part of a "bigger creation" for the world.

I send the biggest hug and kiss to my beloved wife. I send my love to the entire family and friends I met while I was on earth. I visit my wife often in dream state and take her on special journeys with me. She feels my presence around her and I speak gently in her ear at times just to inspire and encourage her that there truly is life after we cross over. My love for her is endless and I am so grateful for her love and devotion to me beyond the call. I will always be here for her as she was for me.

I wish to send my gratitude to Bette Midler for her beautiful music, which has uplifted and inspired many for so long. She has been "the wind beneath the wings" for many through her talents and heart. The vibrations of her music uplift many, as do many other great musicians and artists. "God is surely watching from a distance." I send to her the golden wings of spirit and to all great musicians and artists with their beautiful music that heals and lifts all souls.

I want my friends to know I have a grand time here in other dimensions. There is so much to learn in the many schools of the etheric.

Remember, life does flash by quickly; get your priorities straight; be true to yourself, loved ones, and the rest will take care of itself. When one's focus is service for others, in alignment with higher purpose, then fulfillment comes forth. I did have a feeling of fulfillment when I left, but I short-circuited my life with smoking. So I say, think twice and know the body is a temple; honor it and it will honor you.

Therefore, "I'm so glad we had this time together, and before you know it, comes the time we have to say so long....."

**Johnny Carson's Power Key for Career Success**

**DILIGENCE**
Delight in the career of your passion
Ignite your dreams with focused vision
Let yourself have fun and laughter in life
Initiate connection with mentors and role models
Generous giving to others will return to you
Exercise your personal power and courage
New perspectives will invigorate you
Connect with those who inspire and support you
Energize your dreams through contemplation

**Johnny Carson's Visualization for Success.**

Envision yourself sitting under a star-filled full moon night as you tune into the brightest glistening star. Begin to visualize an iridescent crystalline fountain of light beaming through you as you begin breathing in 5 counts, holding 5 counts and releasing 5 counts for each breath throughout the 10-minute visualization process. As you go more deeply within, envision the golden full moon beam saturating every cell of your being, opening up all your creative centers to tune in to a special project or career dream you have. Breathe out any doubts or fears and let them dissolve in the yellow golden light. See the full project or dream on a screen in front of you and see it expanding to a greater vision than you had imagined. Let the vision come into your heart center and become one with it. Then envision the entire earth enveloped in the yellow golden light of creativity and wisdom saturating every cell of every being, bringing them to higher awareness to fulfill a greater role for humanity. See all in full creativity potential for the highest good of all. See arts, music flourishing as never before, and new creations for helping the planet. Breathe in total success for yourself and all others. Give thanks and it is done.

**AFFIRMATION: I AM DILIGENT IN MY CAREER and LIFE SUCCESS**

*The Best to All,*
*Johnny Carson.*

# Chapter 5

## *Afterlife Wisdom of Jackie O. Kennedy*

### *Connection with Jackie O. Kennedy in Spirit*

Jackie also first "flashed in" during the late 1990's at times when I needed extra courage and empowerment. Once when I was preparing for a special TV interview, she was there beside me just before I went on, smiling and beautiful in an iridescent robe. She told me my work of inspiring others who needed help along their path was priceless. I became very calm and focused and the interview went very well. She, too, like JFK, has appeared at patriotic holidays to sustain the focus for Justice and Freedom for all. She told me she, like JFK, had played many roles as royalty in past lives to prepare her for that role as First Lady. Jackie always appears in a lavender/violet gown (Liberty & Freedom) with a crown, waving a beautiful violet scepter in her right hand. It has been an honor to be in her presence and receive her messages for the world.

Discourse with Jackie O. Kennedy in Spirit - Self-Empowerment

Q. What was your mission while on earth and now in the celestial realms?
A. I am so pleased to be here with you. (Vision shown: she held out her hand to send her greeting to all.) I am here with JFK and this communication is to inspire greater self-empowerment. I speak now to the world that was loving and welcoming to me as the "first

lady." So, it is to the many who were interested when I was in the body that I now speak once again. Now I come to you as a lady of light and I work in the Violet Flame Legions (Freedom and Justice). I am speaking for the empowerment of the American people and the world, that as a whole they may come to awaken to the truth of who they are as individuals of consciousness. This is a time of coming together so that they can create a better world for each person and for humanity as a whole.

We see from these realms there is much cleaning up to be done, so to speak, and many old paradigms are being overturned to new thoughtforms. Few there are who have the conviction and courage to choose the highest good to fight for it. I held the role of holding the light when I was First Lady and much was done to help others.

There are many discouraged in the world today and so we speak to them to encourage them to hold strong to their true convictions of fairness and justice. We come forth with these words that you may know and feel there is a great victory right around the corner. It is holding that torch of light; as in the Olympics, just as one comes close to the great goal, this is when faith must be the strongest. I am speaking in symbolism today for the Olympic athletes know the importance of holding their vision and focus to achieve that victory. Yes, I also had strong affinity with ancient Greece; it holds many truths and secrets of understanding for humankind today.

I help many who have lack of self-esteem, especially women. Many who have great gifts need to step up to the plate and become the true leaders they are meant to be, leading this world into peace, harmony and balance. I am here as a mentor, so to speak, to inspire and uplift others.

**Q. What advice do you have for empowerment of Women in roles as leaders?**

A. When I was playing the role as Jackie, I was blind. I ignored important signs and pushed issues under the carpet. Over time, it caught up with me and I became ill.

One cannot sweep inner conflicts "under the rug" without consequences. The most important key I bring forth is that of inner communication with the self for true empowerment. When one loses that inner solitude and communication, it is easier to go into denial and create illusions. For instance, when one is in a negative, unbalanced or abusive relationship, there comes a turning point when that individual needs to face reality and make a choice. When reality hits home, the choices are always shown very clearly. If the relationship is holding you back, it is no longer serving your highest good or your loved ones, and it is time to move on. I had difficulties in my marriage; however I had chosen to see them through and at the time of JFK's death, we were in harmony with one another. I recommend fully opening to inner communications with the Self through simple meditations, mind talk and prayers. This is crucial to open to the part of Self that has closed down. Also, seeking alignment with the right confidant or advisor is important to help accelerate the process of self introspect. In addition, keeping a journal each day will unfold truth and solutions. The situation will shift and you will move into a new chapter of your life. Write letters of forgiveness to all those you need to, write out all the emotions you wish to release, and burn the letters. You will be relieved and uplifted.

Remember, that when one "chapter of your life" closes, another will open to greater blessings. One might say my life was very colorful and my life had many chapters. I found being out on the water contemplative. Water represents the emotions and the spirit of life, it is transforming, so go to the lakes, rivers or oceans nearby and contemplate there. Do this often as nature "soothes the soul." In this way, you will come to know the next steps for your life so you can open new doorways.

Many feel some doors are closed to them. There are always other choices and these can be opened easily with greater inner communication with the Self, for the universe is unlimited. It is the inner communication that many have shut off for so long that creates the void or block.

I come forth to bring awareness today through use of the Blue Flame Light (Communications) and the Violet Flame Light (forgiveness and freedom). As you come into awareness of clear inner communication and forgiveness of self and others, then you can open to new beginnings in life. I address this also to many parents who do not listen to themselves or their children.

Many children become depressed and lost in the shuffle as no one cares to hear them. Children are calling out for encouragement and nurturing. They have forgotten themselves; perhaps never knew how to nurture themselves. Most of all they have lost touch with true soul purpose and why they came into this life. Once this is regained, all joy and balance is restored.

**Q. If you knew what you knew now, how would you have lived your life differently?**

A. I would have been a stronger spokesperson in the White House for empowerment, women's rights and the good of all. I would have spoken out more on programs for health and environment.

I would have supported more humanitarian projects instead of being projected as a figurehead; I see my role could have had stronger influence for the greater good had I been more awake to my true Self. I would have been seeking my own enlightenment more through inner contemplation and spiritual study. I would have encouraged more foundations to inspire women as leaders and policy makers.

JFK was a great seer and policy maker, but he was out of balance physically. I would have helped him to find the most advanced holistic healers, therapists to assist him back to full strength. We both saw many things that needed to be done for the people; he had a sincere care for the good of humanity and he played a great role, acting from his heart as he could. The world grieved so deeply for his loss because they saw that glimmer of the Master that he was.

In the end, we work together again and he applauds me as a Leader in these realms. We had been royalty together before in Europe in another lifetime and so we played our parts well together. We did the best we could to inspire and enlighten humanity. Now our roles continue in the celestial realms in a greater way to help humanity come into its true Power and Freedom.

**Q. What message do you have for Caroline?**

A. I am here with her extending my arms in admiration of the great inspiration she is to her family, her peers, and the world. I applaud her wonderful authorship and see her in greater public speaking roles that will help a great many people, especially women. She is the Light of my Heart. John Jr. is also here beside me to send her a teddy bear hug, a wink and a double bouquet of roses; keep up the great work; we are so proud of you. All our love and always we are with you (Jackie and JFK Jun).

### Jackie O' Kennedy's Power Key to Self Empowerment

CONFIDENCE
Connect with your Higher Power
Own your decisions
Never give up on your dreams
Forget the mistakes of the past and move on
Identify your strengths and build on them
Deal with issues as they arise and transcend them
Establish a vision for yourself and the world
Never give up your power to anyone
Contact mentors and advisors for support
Elevate yourself to greater achievements

### Jackie O' Kennedy's Self- Empowerment Visualization

Visualize yourself walking up a beautiful crystal stairway. As you reach the top, enter a room filled with Violet Iridescent Light with a throne in the center made of crystal. Continue a cyclical breathing of 7 counts, holding 7 counts and releasing 7 counts throughout the 10-minute visualization. Be seated on the throne and begin to feel a powerful beam of Violet Flame Light pour through every cell of your being. See a beautiful golden crown being placed on your head and a golden scepter in your right hand. See a curtain opening in front of you and see the new vision of your life and the world manifesting. Let all the past dissolve in the violet light and see only the new creations. Become one with these visions and give gratitude for all. Affirm your full empowerment in all arenas of your life for the highest good.

AFFIRMATION: I AM CONFIDENT AND EMPOWERED FOR UNLIMITED SUCCESS

*All my best always,*
*Jackie (Vionna)*

# Chapter 6

## *Afterlife Wisdom of President John F. Kennedy*

### *Connection with JFK in Spirit*

My encounter with JFK came in the late 1990's when he would appear and inspire me, especially on patriotic holidays like President's Day, Memorial Day and Fourth of July. He would "flash" in always very briefly, yet profoundly, in Violet colored suits, reminding me to remember to hold the vision of Justice, Freedom and Peace for the planet. He often indicated that he was working as an overseer with government leaders and policy makers to help restore integrity and effective leadership for America and the world. He told me he worked in the Legion of The Violet Flame of Freedom along with many others. He said when the time was right he would have messages for the world.

Discourses from JFK in Spirit - Justice & Leadership

Q. What is your mission in the afterlife?
A. It is known by all that when it is time to leave the body, a doorway opens; the door opened very brightly for me. It was my soul's choice to leave at that time, although it was a shock at first to my physical and emotional body. I was held back from fully ascending immediately by all the millions of grieving people on earth in confusion. After a short while, some great golden angels came and lifted me into the higher dimensions. There was so much more I wanted to do as President,

and, yet, I was shown on a screen what my life mission was (to inspire world freedom through America (I AM Race). I was also shown what I had accomplished; what I still needed to learn; and how my work would continue in a higher way in the celestial realms. I had "set the stage" while on earth for a much higher mission that continues infinitely. We watch over to insure the Divine Plan is followed through; there are many intense issues at hand, so I come this day to inspire and let all know life does go on and we are eternal beings.

I want to inspire the people of America and the world to see the good in themselves and know they are making a difference. Most importantly, I want people to speak out on what is right and know justice will prevail. All of this takes time.

Along with others in the Violet Flame Legions, I oversee and assist world leaders, politicians and policy makers to inspire and guide them in accordance with the Universal Laws of Cause & Effect; Law of Karma; Law of Return; Law of Forgiveness; Law of Clarity; Law of Free Will; Law of Belief; Law of Reciprocity. We work from these realms to assist in raising all into higher alignment with these laws. The old archaic way of doing things has been cleansed away. A new template is in place for more enlightened souls to be in positions of power in all government structures.

The star children shine brightly as they are the true leaders of the new world and we are helping them to put new systems in place for world peace and harmony. Although all seems in chaos, the 11th hour approaches and the masses will awaken and heaven on earth will prevail for all. Sometimes things appear darkest at the climax of great changes, but it is at these times that even greater faith and courage are needed. These discourses are spoken to encourage all to "ask not what the world can do for you, but what you can do for the world."

**Q. How would you have lived your life differently, now that you know what you know?**

A. I would have taken better care of myself emotionally and physically. I would have searched for the best holistic assistance to find the core issues of my physical problems instead of turning to medications. I would have followed a more in-depth spiritual path of prayer and meditation, seeking advisors and healers to assist me. I would have healed and transcended deep emotional wounds so I could have been a more devoted husband and father for my family. I would have danced and played more and noticed the sweetness of life in the body, for it is so sweet; cherish it in every moment for time passes quickly, my friends.

I would have been more patient in my policy changes. As the saying goes, "Rome wasn't built in a day." Many new policies that first met with resistance would have gradually been accepted. I would have taken more precautions for my own protection.

There is still much discussion about the conditions of my passing over. I wish all to know that the higher outcome of my death was to shift people to open up more to true Freedom. They took many of my quotes and replayed them in their minds and moved forward to reflect on all the important impressions I had left - to be strong, courageous and confident. My mission, though short-lived, created a great shift. The "dark forces" that ended my life in the body, played out a role which in the end revealed Justice and Freedom. I ask you to remember the good that I did, the inspiration I gave and the truths that I upheld for America and the world.

**Q. In order to inspire change in the world, what could you say to inspire others to be greater leaders?**

A. As one seeks balance and alignment within one has greater power and focus to achieve greater goals and victories. Through inner cleansing, contemplation and visualizing, one is not stuck in lower material and self-serving aspects.

When the ego is transcended, all is balanced out according to the universal law of manifestation - all thought creates reality and what goes around comes around. When a leader in any arena makes decisions from self-serving ideals, victory is not achieved for the highest good. When one gets it Right in accordance with universal law, one knows total fulfillment and reaps great rewards in both this life and the afterlife. From these realms, we are working to change the mindset of earthly leaders who are not ruling from the heart for the highest good of all. It is the vibration of higher thought forms, of purification and peace, that transcend discord caused by ignorance of universal laws.

It is said that when pure Light is present, all darkness melts away. Therefore, all should visualize Violet Flame light diminishing all discord and darkness on this planet; this will accelerate the process. Those who cannot make the shift into higher vibrations will take their leave to go to other realms. As if the mother would make way for a new birth to take place, so it is for Mother Earth.

Send compassion to souls still in greed and hatred and see all negative energy changed into generosity, peace, love, balance and harmony for decisions and actions that benefit the highest good for all.

I encourage all leaders to open to inner contemplation and peaceful solutions on the planet. This will offset and dispense negative energies and darkness. Remember that only Light is real; all else is shadow so hold strong to your daily vision of Peace on Earth, for this will accelerate the manifestation of the "New Earth."

**Q. What would you say to world and military leaders about war?**

A. I would say "rethink your strategies for real peace," for you are surrounded by a power far greater than yourselves. Observe the roles you play and know that no action goes unnoticed in universal law and adverse actions that interfere with free will and the highest good of humanity will have repercussions. No action goes without consequence and in the universal light that there is only one infinite power. Thinking that one has complete power over others on the earth plane is nothing but an "illusion." This is the most important thing all leaders should know and remember in their walk while on earth.

When all is said and done, everyone is shown on an "etheric computer screen" in the afterlife what their soul mission was, what they accomplished and any adversities they created that affected humanity. Greater service will need to be done in other realms to make amends for negative impacts to humanity and more difficult roles will have to be played out in future lifetimes, to offset the adversities created. True Leaders come to know that the way of Peace is the only true solution for all. Yes, there is a need for basic defense and protection on the Earth plane at this time, but eventually this planet will return to peaceful state of nature with no need for defense, when all nations honor one another and live in peaceful alliance. This is destiny.

If world leaders went on a conscious out-of-body journey around the world they would see the masses of people affected by any adverse decision or action. In addition, if they saw the greater Karmic repercussion in the next life and in other dimensions, there would be an immediate global shift. Sometimes, this is seen in dream state, but often not remembered consciously. As in “what goes around, comes around,” we say unto you, Karmic Retribution is coming forth much faster because of Mother Earth’s changes; she no longer tolerates fleas that cling to her back.

As you work with each other, open your hearts to techniques of higher understanding of attunement and balance. This is when the great surrender comes and all the solutions for peace unfold in the realization comes that no one has any power over another. Leadership from a clear heart will always be the most successful.

**Q. What message do you have for Caroline?**

A. I would like to send her the biggest hug from my heart. I want her to know I am the proudest a father could be of all she has accomplished within herself and her contributions to the world. She is one of the strongest and most courageous women on the planet. In addition, she is never alone for I am often with her and the family, especially when called upon, overseeing gently as a father does.

I know she often feels my presence around her, as well as Jackie and John Jr., who send their love and hugs. We sometimes visit with her in dream state and take her on beautiful journeys with us. She is a great inspirational author and speaker and will play greater roles in public speaking in the future. I send my unending love and devotion to her and the entire family always and forever.

**John F Kennedy's Power Key to Leadership and Excellence**

**COURAGE**

Communicate with clarity on all levels
Open to unlimited possibilities in all situations
Understand that Excellence comes from Within
Remember to make Decisions in Integrity, for the Highest Good
Appreciate sincerely all those who have helped you
Gather the best alliances and sources for support
Excel in contemplation and visualization for yourself and the world

**John F Kennedy's Leadership Visualization**

Invoke, visualize and breathe in a waterfall pillar of Violet Flame Light, breathing in five counts, holding five counts and releasing for five counts throughout this 10 minute visualization. Contemplate any fears, doubts, regrets, challenges or situations you would like to shift and see them all being transcended to highest outcome. Then visualize the pulsating Violet Flame waterfall enveloping all of your loved ones, friends, and the entire world. Begin to notice densities and negativities lifting. See new inspiration and ideas coming to you for your life and the world. See all world leaders making decisions in integrity for the highest good of all. Affirm; I AM the Violet Flame that transmutes all into justice and victory for the highest good of all. (Note: Strauss waltz music has the vibration of the Violet Flame and can inspire you.) Cross your hands over your heart and bring the Knowingness within that all is done in gratitude.

AFFIRMATION: I AM A LEADER OF INTEGRITY & COURAGE

*Ask not what the world can do for you,*
*but what you can do for the world.*

*My Salute to All,*
*John F. Kennedy (JaNoah)*

# Chapter 7

## *Afterlife Wisdom of Martin Luther King Jr.*

### *Connection with Martin Luther King Jr*

The connection with Martin Luther King has been strongest on the days honoring his memory. Martin Luther King's presence is profound and he sends through a vibration of hope and encouragement to all who can tune into his essence. His message of Freedom and Peace is simple. He often appears in a deep violet suit or robe that is the symbol of forgiveness and freedom. Martin Luther King's wish is for "liberty bells" to ring freely within every heart of humanity. Again, it is an honor and privilege to deliver his discourses.

Discourses from Martin Luther King Jr. in Spirit - Real Freedom

Q. What was your mission on earth and in the afterlife?
A. My mission was and continues to be Global Freedom, justice and peace for humanity. A true sense of freedom within the heart is necessary to attain the soul purpose set forth for each individual. Real freedom also assists in the unification of humanity for the fulfillment of enlightenment and peace.

I work in the Violet Flame Legions (Freedom and Justice) along with John F K. A special dispensation is ringing forth and those beings known as Abraham Lincoln, Thomas Jefferson, George Washington, and several others are gathered here. There are too many to mention as I come forth to speak. I can hear Liberty Bells ring as the "Declaration of Independence" is spoken.

My most important mission is to inspire humanity. Let freedom ring from your hearts in all that you decide and plan. There are many who think they have lost their freedom due to government controls and rigid systems. Remember that freedom always has and always will be your birthright; nothing and no one can take away your soul's true mission or purpose. Freedom and courage go hand in hand. When all seems the most discouraging, this is when a breakthrough will take place to remind all of true freedom and justice.

**Q. Now that you know what you know, what would you have done differently?**
A. I lived my life to the fullest; I see clearly now, the earth is a stage and it was a magnificent role I played, to be a part of helping to balance the karma of humanity - not just for Afro-Americans; but all races and creeds. This work continues here along with millions of others working together in the Legions of the Violet Flame.

**Q. What is your message for the world today?**
A. The founding fathers of America (anagram IAMRACE) set the stage long ago for this nation and the world to bring about the awakening of humanity to real Freedom. The words of the Constitution and Declaration of Independence come from higher dimensions and speak to the hearts and minds of all to honor all human rights. The sacred words in these documents and other documents of Truth came through from the Legions of the Violet Flame (the Freedom Flame) as a template for the world. A great being known as Master St. Germaine oversees this Legion and is devoted to Freedom and Justice for all. He is the one who "mysteriously appeared" during the signing of the Declaration of Independence and shifted the vibrations in the room. Master St. Germaine spoke briefly of the importance that the document be signed as it was ordained from the highest realms for the highest good of all. Master St. Germaine then disappeared as mysteriously as he had appeared.

Since that time, there has been much distraction and digression from the original blueprint - but I come to you this day to announce that the blueprint in the ether has never been offset. My message, in common with many great ones before and after me, was and is to set back into balance that which was out of balance in accordance with universal law. I come today to inspire courage and commitment to uphold the Truths that are self evident for all humanity. This is the time for the planet Earth to reclaim her balance, harmony and strength. All people are now raised knowing that freedom is their birthright through integrity and peace, not battle nor hatred. My mission as Martin Luther King and its continuance is to assist with the release of bondage and despair of all who are blindfolded and do not know they are the Light and Truth.

The legions of the Violet Flame lift many into higher knowing. Much has been done, and is still being done, to offset the discrimination among races and creeds to bring all into Unity according to higher universal law.

Mankind has free will to choose its destiny. The words, "we hold these truths to be self evident, that all men are created equal," are as powerful now as they were then. The Declaration of Independence is a template set forth for all nations, intended for the highest good for all faiths and races. The day will come soon when all nations will come together in Unity and cooperation. This is already decreed from the highest realms for manifestation within the next few years. I come forth to remind all that discrimination is of the past; it only holds society back from its true mission. All should stand forth in Truth and Justice in spiritual attunement in the name of the IAM and principles set forth by the founding fathers. This message comes from the celestial realms to all races, creeds and colors; all are one in essence. It is attunement with the higher self that sets one free. Let Freedom ring loudly within your hearts and minds in knowing you have the power to change all.

We sustain the Freedom Flame with the aim that all of humanity will ascend and be free in the Light that never fails. When everyone realizes that Victory and Freedom is attained with the transcendence of fear and judgment, then the greatest victory reigns.

**Q. What is your message for loved ones?**

A. I send big hugs and kisses to my family. They know I am close by, assisting them gently through their life to inspire them to continue my message and to follow their dreams always. We are together in heart.

## Martin Luther King's Power Key of Real Freedom

### FREEDOM

Forgive past mistakes and injustices
Remember to make decisions with a clear heart
Excel in focused visioning for world harmony
Establish teachings of equality to children
Deliver the message of truth and justice for all
Open to unlimited possibilities and opportunities
Maintain the knowingness for world peace

## Martin Luther King's Freedom Visualization

Envision multi-millions of violet flame liberty bells enveloping your entire being. Breathe in 7 counts, hold 7 counts and release 7 counts throughout this 10-minute meditation. Breathe in the knowing of what true liberty and freedom feels like. This is your birthright. Let these liberty bells saturate every cell in your body, mind and spirit. Envision what the planet looks like in pure peace and freedom for every soul. Let your heart center extend the expanding liberty bells out to the entire world. See planet Earth enveloped in one huge violet flame liberty bell, which rings freely for all to hear. See the new world of all honoring, respecting and helping one another. Clasp your hands together knowing that this is done, and in gratitude.

**AFFIRMATION: I AM THE FREEDOM AND PEACE I SEEK**

*May True Freedom Ring in All Hearts,*
*Martin Luther King (Melkier)*

# Chapter 8

## *Afterlife Wisdom of Princess Grace*

### *Connection with Princess Grace*

Princess Grace came forth to communicate with me for this book especially as she has a specific message to give the world on self-fulfillment. Her presence in a robe and crown of iridescent aquamarine (serenity and clarity) is so profound and it is hoped that all can feel her presence through her special words herein. She indeed emanates grace in all that she is and she opens the doorway for more grace in everyone's life.

Princess Grace's Discourses - Self Fulfillment

Q. What is your mission/role in the afterlife?
A. I am much honored to be with you. I appear in a robe of aquamarine, representing serenity and clarity. I work in the Legions of Grace to help uplift humanity. I am very happy in these realms to assist in soothing the souls of humanity. I work in alliance with others in cleansing the waters and assisting the dolphin and whale kingdoms to do their work in transforming the planet.

Q. What is your message for the women of today?
A. I wish to touch them with a scepter of peace and serenity for so many are stressed and out of touch with inner self. Because of the many great changes on this planet there is much unrest, fear and upheaval. The Serenity Light (Aquamarine) is sent to soothe all.

Many know not how to ask for help as they feel all the changes in their bodies and lives and I work here, among many others, to guide souls. For example, I inspire souls to go to the, lakes, oceans, rivers, and let the waters soothe.

It was my honor to work in the role as Grace Kelly; I played many roles, and the greatest role was that of Princess, for I came to see and understand diplomatic situations and to study these, from a quiet stance, of course. The role I played helped to influence others in doing good and I am told I played my role well for I always sought to have compassion with others. Peace within self brings peace with others. Peace is contagious as fear is.

As peace prevails within oneself, it is easier to envision peace within others and the world. Seek spiritual practices in your life and allow yourself to contemplate what is most important. Sometimes there are physiological reasons why one can't have peace and there is always a solution when one seeks it. It is important to keep the mental, emotional, physical and spiritual body in balance as much as possible. Many are not balanced in emotions, which can be corrected by natural means.

There are so many realms of higher learning here and the physical body is only one aspect of the multidimensional self. True clarity comes when one is in alignment with one's full essence. It is in this clarity that all else can be accomplished.

**Q. What would you have done differently now that you know what you know?**

A. There is not much I would have done differently. I would have been more open and trusting with others. I would have used my platform to make more of a difference in the world. I did accomplish much in my life but I must say I would have smelled more gardenias and taken more time for contemplation while in the body. I left the earth plane seemingly before my time; and yet I speak from these spheres in knowing that I did have great fulfillment in my life, both as an actress in the theaters as well as in the royal partnership (we are rejoined here in spirit).

All in all I had what would be called a fairytale life, and of course it had its challenges, but I always tried to go within to find solace and answers. I valued my solitude when I could have it as it gave me strength. For in the world of chaos and confusion, it is priceless to set time in morning and evening - even just 15 minutes in meditation to visualize your goals. Go to the waters and be at peace there; take part in projects to cleanse the waters of this planet and demand it to be a priority of the governments. The dolphin kingdoms cry out for this as do all nature kingdoms on planet earth.

All of us here who speak these discourses sustain the vision for the restoration of nature and the environment. This restoration is overdue. Time is of the Essence for the sustenance of humanity on this planet.

There are many who have grand plans and ideas for new energy; I say let them come forth and implement them and we send a fountain of aquamarine light to cleanse all of Mother Earth.

**Q. What is the message for your children in the world?**

A. I would like to pass on to them (along with Prince Ranier, who is here by my side), a message to carry my love and inspiration within their hearts, to learn from inspirational mentors and to help the world as they can in their roles. I remind them that to listen and hear others clearly helps one understand others; therein is a gemstone for success and dignity. When it is your time to pass from this world you will know that you absolutely made a difference in the lives of others by following your heart's dreams and goals. This is where the full respect is earned in the end. Let the wisdom of your heart always be your guide. Know I am always here to assist along the way. Take time for inner contemplation in your daily lives, for the rewards are great. Both Prince Ranier and I send all our love unending to you all.

**Q. What advice do you have for world leaders?**

A. From this vantage point, it is clearly seen that decisions to let people be in true democracy rather than bondage, enlightenment rather than ignorance, and justice rather than injustice create the highest good. When one passes over, the soul will know the consequences through karmic balancing of decisions that were not in the highest good of others. In the end, all comes back that has been given through universal law.

To make the best policy decisions, one should seek to fully understand what is best for all and truly oversee with fair and just intent. It is the integrity of intention that sets the stage for the results. Those who are in the illusion of "supreme rule" are mistaken, for nothing goes unnoticed in the universal light. Choose always the highest course of action and for this many rewards will await you.

I, along with many others in these realms, hold a focus for the Department of Peace for all nations that will be implemented within the next few years. This is a great program that will shift the world in all arenas, including the advancement of educational institutions for peaceful conflict resolutions and world serenity.

All great plans take time. We are very patient here and we know Peace is indeed coming in fullness to this planet. All players are in order to bring forth the international Department of Peace and all are encouraged to support it. Peace in the homes, schools, neighborhoods, communities and the world is forthcoming. An international conclave will be organized to oversee and ensure peaceful resolutions are priority. It is so simple but is necessary. The international Department of Peace is an intervention tool to accelerate peace on earth and so it will. All will be balanced out and brought into unification as mother earth is shifting, so all are encouraged to sustain the true Vision for World Serenity and Harmony.

### Princess Grace's Power Key (Self Fulfillment)

CLARITY
Clear Intentions in decision making yield greatest results
Lighten your self-perceptions and see the good in all situations
Allow yourself to forgive and learn from the past
Remember to be true to yourself above all
Initiate new ways of creating a better world
Take time out to play and enjoy the simple things
Yesterday is but a mirror, use it wisely

### Princess Grace's Aquamarine Visualization

Visualize yourself in the center of 7 multi-level fountains of magnificent liquid crystalline aquamarine light (serenity and peace) pouring through every level and dimension of your being. Breathe in 7 counts, hold 7 counts and release for 7 counts throughout this visualization (10 minutes). Set your intentions for total serenity for yourself and the world. Reflect on releasing all the injustices and misconceptions in your life and the world and let them all go into the iridescent aquamarine waterfall of light. Reflect that peacefulness is the natural state of life and allow your mind and emotions to become one with the aquamarine fountain. Begin to feel uplifted and refreshed as the fountain becomes stronger and flows through you into the center of the earth. See the waterfall expanding to the entire country and the world. Allow the clarity of a vision of a serene and joyous world come to you. Stay in contemplation of the new clarity you have created for yourself and the world for 10 minutes. May peaceful waters always flow through your mind, body and spirit now and forever. May total clarity remain, as you cross your hands over your heart.

AFFIRMATION: I AM FULFILLED IN HIGHEST CLARITY

*Peaceful Waters to You,*
*Princess Grace (Lana Grace)*

# Chapter 9

## *Afterlife Wisdom of John Lennon*

### *Connection with John Lennon in Spirit*

John Lennon "flashes in" when his music is on or during television specials about him. John Lennon is a magnificent peacemaker; his mission continues through other musicians and even through people who have a focus for justice and peace on earth. He usually appears in a violet robe (forgiveness and freedom) or a yellow-gold robe (creativity and arts). His discourses are very inspirational for all. His keynote song, of course, is "Imagine."

John Lennon's Discourses - Creating Music & Harmony

Q. What was your mission/role on earth and now, in the afterlife?
A. When I left my body that fateful day in shock, wondering why this happened to me, many great angels lifted me into the Golden Light. I was shown on a screen of light that the one who had done this was not in a balanced consciousness, or it would not have happened. I came to know it was a karmic balance from other lifetimes and this individual was playing a role. It was my time to take my leave and move on to higher dimensions and from these realms I inspire others

in music and wisdom.

I have simple words for the world, for the solutions of life are simple. Peace is indeed coming to this world. It is a time of Renaissance and many are being led to the true light. It is in imagining that the creation of change happens. One must begin to think in terms of positive creation. It is in co-creating the highest form of intention that correct action can then affect the whole of everything. From these realms, as in the body, I assist in awareness of creating harmony and balance for the world. Many of us in the Legions of Freedom and Will, work together to radiate humanity for its evolution to higher consciousness.

When I was in the body, I saw the need for change and so I brought this through music, as do many. The songs, which contain messages for humanity, were a great service. My message for all musicians and artists is to plant seeds for uplifting and creating a better world. Sustain the knowing of what you want to create for a better world and the words/lyrics will come to you. There is a divine plan for this planet and it is unfolding for all. Do not look back on others; set the intentions for the new; focus on the changes you wish to make and these intentions will go forth and blossom.

**Q. What inspired the words and music of "Imagine" and other music?**

A. The words came through as inspired from spirit, from higher dimensions, as did all of my music and that of the Beatles. It came through from an intention to create a peaceful and harmonic earth, to inspire humanity rather than discourage it. In these realms, I now take part in inspiring others in the same way. We are all spirit, just taking part a short time in the body. When one knows this, a sense of true understanding begins. One opens to receive communion with higher dimensions through inner contemplation. In these realms there are music, theater, actor, and artists' guilds just as there are on earth. Life goes on in a glorious way and I am here as testimony!

I would not encourage any type of addictions, especially drugs and alcohol which short circuit the system and eventually cause destruction of one's life. Rather it is spiritual flow of attunement with higher self that brings through higher creativity. I did receive celestial visions when I was living (such as Mother Mary), and she inspired much music. I kept my gifts of inner vision and inner hearing to myself. Gifts of spirit should be shared with others for they are natural; remember, the body is only one part of being. Now, along with others in these realms, I inspire musicians and artists who wish to make a difference in the world.

It is fine-tuning of spiritual gifts through meditation and inner healing, with techniques to quiet the mind, that will enhance your gifts. This is where the greatest inspiration comes; all spiritual masters know this. I especially have a focus with musicians and artists who are gifted and I help them tune in to their higher self to achieve greater good for the planet through the arts.

**Q. Would you share more about the consequences of addictions in respect to creativity?**

A. Yes, drugs are a shortcut believed to help enlightenment; but I tell you surely there are no shortcuts as they say. Drugs and alcohol have an adverse affect on the brain and physical body. Prolonged use circumvents them from connecting with higher vibrations. Over time, it is destructive and destroys the brain cells; the auric field is torn, sometimes irreparably, and this affects one's whole life.

Therefore, I say to you why not shift to natural forms of high though meditation and seek great teachers and healers? There are many who can assist you in transcending addictions that hold the soul back from its true path.

Drug and alcohol addictions cause physical, emotional, and mental damage and eventually death; then the balance needs to be found on other dimensions. Your body has the ability to tune in to natural forms of enthusiasm and joy to bring through the spiritual gifts you have. Being true to yourself is most important.

**Q. What is your message for the world today?**

A. Create from your heart and soul; not from only from the mind. You are the creator of your destiny; know that this life in the body is a very special gift; let it unfold and follow your special gifts and talents in contribution to humanity. When you feel your creativity is blocked, ask for assistance and you will receive it from the right source. You will experience the greatest fulfillment when you follow through and create your true purpose. Then everything in your life will shift to greater health, wealth, grace and peace.

**Q. Would you like to share a message for Paul McCartney?**
A. I would like to say it was a great honor to work with such a soul again (as we had several lifetimes together, one as brothers). We played our roles together well and created incredible music with the group. We knew our presence was making a great difference in the world then and still is today. I oversee and assist him from time to time as a brother would. I would like to say that his work and devotion to others is remarkable and he has a great heart and is a great giver to humanity. I am alive and well and very much in much joy in these realms.

I send him and all the Beatle members my blessings and encouragement in continuance of work for the greater good of all.

**Q. If you knew what you know now, how would you have lived your life differently?**
A. I would have been more compassionate to my body and taken better care of myself; I did some reckless things and to honor and respect the physical self is so important. I would have spoken out more for world peace and humanitarian causes and I would have formed more foundations to help the world in charitable ways. I would have taken more time for my own enlightenment. All in all, I would have been more compassionate with others. I would have liked to be an ambassador and helped youth not to get involved in the addiction scene.

**Q. What is your message for Yoko?**
A. I wrap my arms around her and I send her a triple bouquet of yellow roses. I send unending gratitude and blessings for the continuance of my legend's message to the world. I know she feels my presence with her always.

**Q. Do you have a special message for the world?**
A. Keep imagining and holding the vision of world peace and harmony; keep the focus of thought and intention for the highest good and it will be done; as above so below, heaven on earth.

Keep following your dreams. Imagine a grand new world in perfect harmony, cooperation, alliance, nurturing, abundance, joy and love.

**John Lennon's Power Key (Creating Music & World Harmony)**

**IMAGINE**

Imagine a world without war and conflict
Music of the heart and soul lifts all
Allow your music of the heart to be heard
Gather friends who share your own ideals and values
Initiate groups for contemplation on world peace
Now is the time to create your music or artistic talents
Emerge with highest visions for all

**John Lennon's Creative Visualization**

Prepare for a minimum 10-minute meditation and visualization. As you breathe in 8 counts, hold 8 counts and release 8 counts, begin to see yourself immersed in crystalline violet light rays pouring through every part of your being as you release all resentment, regrets, anger, fear, mistrust and misunderstandings. Feel yourself coming into a feeling of forgiveness and letting go of all issues that surround you. As the violet light saturates your entire being, see it going out to all loved ones, friends, your community and the rest of the world for forgiveness. Then begin to see a radiance of yellow golden light in the form of a figure "*8" (infinity) pouring through above you into every cell of your being and as you continue to breath, see a new level of creative energy open up at your solar plexus for your own musical or artistic gifts. Send this out to the world and see the whole planet being bathed in creative light to awaken all to their potential. Now see the entire planet in a peaceful state of oneness with no war, conflicts, disease, pollution, deprivation, poverty or lack. See only that of total harmony and sharing. Now listen for the beautiful angelic music you hear and rejoice.

AFFIRMATION: I NOW IMAGINE AND SEE THE WORLD IN PEACE

*Peace and Harmony to all,*
*John Lennon*

# Chapter 10

## *Afterlife Wisdom of Howard Hughes*

### *Connection with Howard Hughes in Spirit*

Howard Hughes has "flashed" in from time to time during the last ten years and he was especially present, inspiring the writing of this chapter, when I saw his movie "Aviator." During the movie, special inspiration of his message to the world came through. Howard Hughes is a great guide to many who open to his essence for business and prosperity. He has been a great inspiration to me for confidence in business matters. He always appears in a bright golden suit with golden shoes and top hat (symbolizing abundance and infinity).

Howard Hughes' Discourses - Financial Wealth

Q. What is your mission/role in the afterlife?
A. (He appears smiling in his shimmering golden suit in a golden archway) I assist in the Legions of Abundance to teach and inspire humanity how to open the doorway to infinite wealth and prosperity in all arenas of life. I also assist with shifting group consciousness on the planet to unlimited sources of abundance. The famous words, "be in this world, but not of it," help one to remember not to be attached to the third dimensional world. Detachment is a great lesson we assist many with on the earth plane. I come to remind all that the earth is indeed a stage and it is important to maintain thoughts that raise above all the obstacles third dimensional life has, to be successful in any venture in conscious thought.

**Q. What guidance do you have for attaining financial independence?**

A. Consistent conscious projected thoughts of peace, harmony and prosperity directly leads to financial independence. It has been proven by organizations on the planet that the vibrations of thought affect outcome (see David Hawkins books and heartmath.com). It has also been evidenced that all discordant thoughtforms can be transmuted and transcended to higher levels of creativity and abundance. The famous scientist/inventor known as Nicola Tesla works with lightning energies that help to ignite and empower humanity into higher realities. I also work with him at times to help humanity develop the means of using natural resources for power. Solar power and natural means are available when humanity is ready for higher technologies. This level of knowing brings forth the KNOWING that all abundance comes from the source and is infinite. It is only the conscious mind that has adopted negative programming of lack and limitations that holds humanity back from realizing its full potential as light beings and infinite creators.

The lightning blue radiance can also be used to manifest and create abundance through the power of Will and Faith.

I do not have a lot to say but some words of wisdom. I share gratitude to those blessed souls who brought forth the recent movie about my life. Leonardo DiCaprio, who has an attunement with me, received the call from these realms to bring forth the "golden globe" production to inspire the world through my life. The movie served as a great activation for the masses to remind them that maintaining personal power is necessary for achieving visions and dreams. It also reminded all not to be set back by obstacles and to be confident in the face of adversities. It had the effect of helping many souls open to their artistic gifts and follow their dream projects. It was my intent that the movie would inspire humanity to achieve its highest potential without allowing others' beliefs to hold them back. I had a mission to help accelerate the air transportation and movie industries and my soul knew this needed to be accomplished regardless of the obstacles.

I also "see" now from these realms that I had a group spirit council of masters that worked with me in that lifetime as my "team." All souls have a "spirit team" that works with them from the time they come into the body; some have a greater team than others, depending on the soul's mission. My spirit team greatly assisted me in all the projects, protected me and even helped when I had health problems. It was always my higher mind through which the genius for the creations manifested. Higher mind or Divine mind knows all things on all levels, so the more attuned one is, the greater the achievements.

In that life, Archangel Michael was my protector and helped me a great deal in overcoming my many physical limitations. So, in the end, my spirit team and I achieved great victories for humanity's progression and showed how the impossible was made possible. Manifestation is always a flowing current; it is the lower mind and emotions that get in the way of the flow. Let the rivers of endless abundance flow through you and all others.

**Q. What would you have done differently now that you know what you know?**

A. First of all, no matter what the physical imbalance is in the body, when you seek the higher power for your path, this alignment will create the peace you need to achieve your goals effortlessly. It is through inner work, contemplation and meditation that the full source of knowing and creating can manifest. I closed myself off from others, as you all know. I was embarrassed of who I was. I had been caught from any early age in an abusive situation and was not fully aware of the source of my difficulties. All is forgiven now and I have transcended that karma for all other embodiments.

I speak to all those who abuse children, in any way on any level, that it does comes back to you in the Karmic Law of Cause and Effect, "what goes around comes around." I also speak to anyone who is abusing anyone in any way. This will return to you; for what you do unto others does return to you on earth, is compensated through special service in the afterlife, or another lifetime. Seek your own inner healing through therapy, counseling and spiritual sources. Knowledge and application of the universal law of forgiveness is essential. Through the many discourses in this book, we in the celestial realms wish to convey the importance of understanding and following the universal laws that govern all of humanity.

I would have achieved much more in that lifetime had I trusted enough to find holistic healing. In those days doctors just gave medication for the physical, which did not help. I tried so hard to prove I was worthy of being loved. I felt the absence of love within myself. It is so important first and foremost to love yourself. I wish to commend Leonardo and the whole staff for "Aviator," for conveying the truth and inspiring all those who watched it. It won a "golden globe" award from these realms as well as on earth!

I always tried to see the bigger picture in business; see always beyond the hurdles of life and it will serve you.

Treat your competition with courtesy and gratitude, for they can help you to soar. In the end when it is time for you to leave the body you will see that you learned and rose above lessons and challenges and most of all that you did your best.

**Q. What is your guidance for attaining wealth?**

A. Remember that "plugging into the universal light socket" daily is essential and all wealth is in the "I" of the beholder. Apply the Golden Rule in all arenas, for all that is given in fairness, justness and generosity, returns in unlimited ways to you.

You are the source of all - do not depend on others for your abundance; when you truly know this in your heart, you will have continuous prosperity. There is always enough to go around so release beliefs of lack and limitation. One can learn this through teachers and counselors who can accelerate the process. Bless and congratulate others in their success and your success will be greater. Remember you have the power to create your highest potential and contribute to the world in the greatest way. The universe is a huge computer program; delete the past records that no longer serve and set the programs for the continuum of infinite giving, receiving and fulfillment. Wealth is a state of mind. Affirm your own millionaire consciousness in body mind, and spirit. The wealth of spirit brings all other wealth.

The aspect of deserving which affects so many can be addressed by affirming that it is your birthright to have wealth on all levels. The value you place within yourself is the value of infinite abundance.

You are the value that you seek, unlimited.

Open the doorway to the infinite power that you are and have always been. Open the treasure chest of your hearts and see that it is all there. When you are following your dreams, all the obstacles will fall away. Keep the compassion and light with others. Respect them and they will respect you. Be patient with them and they will be patient with you. Be compassionate with them and they will be compassionate with you. Go forth with highest and clearest intentions and all will unfold for you.

**Q. If you knew what you know now, how would you have lived your life differently?**

A. I would have taken more time for inner healing and enjoyed more quiet time for inner reflection. I would have found holistic therapies and spiritual healing that could have helped my imbalance and mental anguish. I would have opened to fully heal rather than sweep my shortcomings under the rug. The deep wounds kept me from seeing the higher truth I needed for peace within myself and so outer achievements were my focus.

I say to seek your own enlightenment then the career and business will take care of itself; it is never too late to find the balance. Many beings in these realms work with souls that are open to bring through creative ideas to help heal the environment, through great technologies and through genius. All comes forth in Divine Mind.

All have this potential and all are one with the higher spark of light and every soul is a star. Shine that star brightly and awaken now; don't settle for less than what you deserve and listen to others who have wisdom for you. It is important not to buy into the illusion you know it all, for then you can lose it all.

When you know in you heart of hearts that something is important to bring forth, hold the course firmly, the connections you need will open. Hold fast to the vision for yourself and the world. Speak up for what you firmly believe in; make allies of your enemies; and treat all as you would like to be treated (the golden rule). Persistent focused strength, conviction and faith bring one to the highest goal sooner. Create from integrity, and you will achieve unlimited wealth and prosperity in all arenas of life.

### Howard Hughes' Power Key for Financial Wealth

**WISDOM**

Wealth is in the "I" of the beholder - it is within you
Infinite source of abundance flows through all
See only the highest manifesting for yourself and the world
Dissolve negative beliefs, lack and limitations on all levels
Open to Knowing you can create unlimited prosperity now
Manifesting is allowing the universal flow through you

### Howard Hughes Abundance Visualization

Visualize Golden Waterfalls (the size of Niagara Falls or bigger) flowing through you as you breathe in for 8 counts, hold for 8 counts and release for 8 counts throughout this visualization (10 minutes). Begin you feel one with the infinite source to create projects for unlimited wealth flowing through you as the waterfalls dissolve all your fears of lack and allow multi-millions of golden nuggets and dollars flow into your hands and bank account. Synchronize this vision with seeing ten percent or more of your wealth going out to foundations of the world needing your charitable contributions. Begin to see all deprived people being fed, clothed, educated, housed and placed in worthy jobs. See now the golden waterfalls of abundance increasing through you in the form of "multiple figure 8's" (infinity) and going out to the world in a perfect circle of energy. Envision the entire planet engulfed in these magnificent golden waterfalls of prosperity in all arenas of life including the environment, air and waters. Visualize the world in total harmony and abundance shared with all. Now see your abundance increasing in unlimited ways - the more you are giving, the more you are receiving. Allow new and creative ideas for greater abundance to flow throughout the world. You are the abundance you seek - millionaire consciousness physically, mentally, emotionally and spiritually.

**AFFIRMATION: I AM ABSOLUTE CONTINUUM OF WEALTH AND ABUNDANCE IN HARMONY WITH THE WORLD, AND SO IT IS, DONE DEAL!**

*Here's to Your Infinite Abundance,*
*Howard Hughes (Helia)*

# Chapter 11

## *Afterlife Wisdom of Elizabeth Montgomery*

### *Connection with Elizabeth Montgomery in Spirit*

Elizabeth Montgomery (Samantha on "Bewitched"), has appeared to me often during the past several years. She always "flashes in" dressed in a peach-colored gown (symbolizing enthusiasm and joy) with a crown on her head and scepter in her right hand, winking at me and smiling. She has often "flashed in" to verify my judgment in situations of discernment with others and to uplift, much like the character she played as "Samantha" in Bewitched. Elizabeth has also conveyed messages during my consultations with others who relate to her "magical nature." Her lightness of heart will inspire you as you read her beautiful discourses. Elizabeth reminds all that all barriers can be overcome and that perceptions can change in an instant, if we choose!

Discourses with Elizabeth Montgomery in Spirit

Q. What is your mission/role in the afterlife?
A. Hello Sweethearts, I am so pleased to be with you once again. I work in these realms in the Legions of enthusiasm and joy that is the color of creation and unfolding potential (peach). When I was living my life I tried to maintain an attitude of optimism - that is so important, because what one projects with the mind is what one creates. I am

here to remind all of the magical presence of life itself.

In the role as Samantha, I always tried to show symbols of power in oneself as I was the one who came up with solutions to the problems and obstacles that arose. We can, in the snap of a finger or the blink of an eye, change our thoughts, our actions and the outcome of any situation.

I come to work with others in jubilance to help them shift their way of thinking; it is a great joy to work with others in this way; and for many stuck in the illusion of life in the body, there is so much more to know. We work in these Legions to help humanity open and experience more joy in everyday life by "seeing" the bigger picture of life itself. I come to remind all that there truly is much more beyond the body; you are spirit and from this magic does occur. All supernatural gifts are gifts of spirit. I help infuse people with a new spark of enthusiasm to help them create and live their true potential.

**Q. What is your message for the women of today?**

A. I remind them not take themselves so seriously. It is the childlike sense of joy and exuberance that moves one into the success and full empowerment they seek. I would like to inspire young women especially, and those preparing for higher education; I advise them to set their goals early and write them out in a sacred book, reflect on them daily, fine-tune them and ensure they will manifest in a greater way. Remember that you can play any role you wish and not settle for a career that seems easier or a role you "should" be playing. In the end you will be that much more fulfilled and so will your loved ones. Never give up your dreams for others; compromises do need to be made, but it is important to follow through with your hearts' desires.

That is what magic is - knowing, believing and allowing the unfolding of what you have projected. Inner work and meditations are most important; the more you learn from those who can take you through doorways of awakening, the better your life will be. Divine Magic happens in an instant. See beyond the obstacles and limitations. You can achieve all you set out to do; it may not manifest in the way you thought, but when one gives up on dreams, it brings great sorrow in these realms for they have closed down a part of themselves. Spiritual alignment and attunement is important to keep all the centers open and flowing in the body. So this simple message is to always keep the sense of enthusiasm in every aspect of your life. When obstacles arise, remember with the snap of your fingers and the twitch of your nose you can instantly change your perception and thus, your reality.

Choose now to change fear into courage; doubt into knowing; lack into prosperity; sadness into joy; anger into laughter; denial into acceptance; anxiety into peace; regret into relief; and despair into joy. Thought can change all things in an instant; thoughts can be measured, and positive thoughts have high vibration, negative ones a lower vibration. The higher the vibration, the greater the manifestation.

So my message to all, including the children, is to keep your thoughts high above the clouds for it is in this way Divine Magic occurs. All is unfolding for you, sweethearts. All the talents you have are unlimited. You are all Divine Magical Beings that can truly soar in the realms of perception and creation.

**Q. Now that you know what you know, what would you have done differently?**

A. The most important thing in life is to love and be loved and I had this in my life. Although my life seemed short, it was full; and I must say it was a great joy to play the TV role I did that had such healing power for many in their own lives. The humor lifted many and it does to this day as we "watch the reruns." I loved my film career and had a blessed life with, of course, some obstacles - as do all.

Remember that the earth is the stage and we all play all our roles; play it well for in the end the greatest gift is to fulfill your part the best you can and inspire others, even down to the smile of a child. These are the sweet things of life that I miss. Cherish life for it passes like the snap of a finger. Make a decision now to open a new chapter of optimism in your life and create the fullness of what you came here to do.

I would have taken more time to enjoy the beauty of the earth. I would have, as many other discourses in this book convey, focused more on my spiritual path and evolvement. I see now there are many holistic healing centers to help souls awaken to higher knowing and transcend past issues. I would have traveled more on sacred journeys and I would have shared more with others. In these realms I assist children to open to their creative potential and I would have liked to form organizations to help young people excel in the arts. There are many of us in these realms who are working together with that being known as "Princess Diana" to accelerate a universal educational system on earth to enhance the academic, holistic, artistic and spiritual potential for all children. All children on the planet are Star Children. They are gifted on all levels, much evolved, intuitive, spiritual and light-years beyond their parents. These children are the leaders of the new earth and they will take their lead starting in 2008. There are many books and research on star children (see also *Indigo, Crystal, and Rainbow Children*). We would like to encourage an organizational think tank to assist the star children who are lost and discouraged to help them unlock their true creativity.

There is a grand plan for this planet to help the masses open to their true purpose in being here. It is the spark of enthusiasm and joy that ignites and lifts one into the higher vibrations of creativity. As one door closes, another greater one opens. Remember, all things ARE possible and may laughter always lift you.

## Elizabeth's Power Key of Joyful Manifesting

JOY
Joy and enthusiasm expand creativity
Open to your unlimited potential
You have the innate ability to shift obstacles into opportunities

## Elizabeth's Joyful Manifesting Visualization

Relax into a deep 10-minute meditation while breathing in gently for 8 counts, holding for 8 counts and releasing for 8 counts. Begin to visualize a beautiful fountain of peach crystalline light flowing through you. Allow the peach fountain of light to flow through every cell of your being on all levels and begin to notice a calm, joyous feeling envelop you. Now see a large screen of light in front of you and envision a project you want to manifest within the screen of light. See it becoming larger and larger in full view and envision the full details of this project on the screen as If watching a live movie. Now allow the peach fountain to pour through the screen and see your project becoming fully activated for the highest good of all.

Become one with the screen of light and embrace the feeling of full manifestation of the project. Cross your hands over your heart affirming it is done and all is manifesting in joyfulness and gratitude.

AFFIRMATION: I CREATE SUCCESS IN JOYFUL ENTHUSIASM

*Joyfully and Magically Yours,*
*Elizabeth Montgomery (Shenara)*

# Chapter 12

## *Afterlife Wisdom of Michael Landon*

### *Connection with Michael Landon in Spirit*

Michael Landon has come forth many times in past several years to inspire and give me encouragement on my path and work. The TV show, "Highway to Heaven," was exemplary of his true higher essence and on some level, he says he knew it was a special show for him and it would inspire the world for a long time to come. Michael Landon's basic message is that of self-forgiveness and faith. He often appears in an emerald green suit or robe (symbolizing truth and healing).

The highway to heaven is indeed a beautiful one. At the time of his passing over from cancer, I had sent a special letter of messages for healing and offered my services; he knew this and appeared directly to me shortly after he passed over to thank me, among many others, of course, who had sent their love. His charm and wit come through in his special messages to the world, which he sends forth from his heart to ours.

Michael Landon's Discourses (Miracles)

Q. What is your mission/role in Spirit?
A. I work in the Legions of Truth and Healing (emerald green) and I inspire others to transform their lives through inner healing and growth. The television show "Highway to Heaven" was the greatest service I could give as playing that role taught many lessons to humanity. I

always tried to seek roles that inspired others.

**Q. What message would you like to pass on to humanity about your life in spirit?**

A. There is no real death, only eternal life, and there is much learning and service in these realms. It is most important to be who you really are in life. I was hard on myself and my family and so I make up for this in these realms. I want my loved ones to know I am their guardian angel now watching over them. I extend the Emerald Healing Ray to all my loved ones and to all who call out for healing; many in these dimensions do this with joy. On the screen you can see after you pass over all that you did and could have done and the lessons still to be learned. When one calls on the emerald green healing ray, great waves of purification and healing come forth; peace reigns. One should call upon this ray and ask Archangel Raphael for assistance with healing on all levels. Raphael will always be there along with others in this Legion.

**Q. What do you know now about your illness and healing that you did not know during the cancer?**

A. I had not taken care of myself very well - my diet, bad habits and environment all contributed to my illness, as well as not resolving past issues. Holistic healing is in many forms - massage, acupuncture, eating healthy foods, taking more time out in nature - are important for overall health and wellness. The body is the temple and life is short, so in order to fulfill one's true life purpose and live the fullness of life, one must learn the best holistic way of living. There are many books on wellness and healthy eating to assist. It serves one in the highest way to attend to this.

Also, being flexible and letting things flow easily is important. There are many opportunities to see the truth in one's life. Some of the choices I made for my own health and thinking process were not always the best and I was inwardly quite critical of my weaknesses. Holding on to past regrets serves no purpose, but causes disease in the body. When one seeks the balance emotionally, mentally, physically and spiritually, then all else prevails.

**Q. Now you know what you know, how would you live differently?**

A. I certainly would have taken more time for peaceful nature walks and sharing with others; contributing more to society; not getting so caught up in the Hollywood scene. I would have listened more and when I received the messages to take better care of myself, I would have. I work in these legions to assist others to take better care of health and wellness. There are so many lost souls who need assistance in valuing their life in the body. The emerald green light assists on many levels and it is our honor and joy here to help as we can.

**Q. What is your message about healing oneself?**

A. I would share that being true to oneself is most important, above all. When you receive inner guidance about your health or wellbeing, seek the assistance needed for better health. There are always consequences when the body is out of balance and it will affect one's whole life. These imbalances cause dysfunction and disease. How one thinks and feels affects total wellness.

Being true to oneself sounds simple, but it is not always. It can mean saying no to a situation when the ego would want to go and do that certain thing. It means taking a back seat when you would want to take a front seat. It means telling someone you can't support him or her in a situation as you need to be true to yourself; it means standing alone in your own power when others around you will judge you. It means being true to your higher self, not the lower self that is not always in touch with the highest and best for you. It means taking time for inner contemplation and reflection to know oneself better. It means following your spiritual path, and cleansing negative thoughts and beliefs.

It takes much effort to be true to oneself, but it can be done. Ask and you shall find strength. Affirm absolute healing now and know that the power and presence is already taking place. Miracles take place in an instant. The source of all healing is through spirit. May the emerald fountains of light now shower upon you and through you on all levels and dimensions. Allow the truth to unfold within you and the new growth will awaken within you. The horizon is bright and glorious and the Highway to Heaven surely exists, for I witnessed it as the Crystal Stairway of Light in which there are no bounds. In these realms, all things are possible and all exists simultaneously.

All one does for another is always accounted for and when one helps in the healing of another, unlimited rewards come forth. Help one another and seek the true healing of mind, body, and spirit. It is time to bring heaven to Earth within yourself first!

My love to my beloved family and fans, who sent so much love to me when I passed over. I send back a radiance of the Emerald Green Light and may you always know and feel that light that you truly are. Take care of yourself. Take time to reflect on the important things of life itself. Remember, you are Love in Action in the body, but most of all you are Spirit, a bright shining light that is endlessly loved by the celestial realms.

### Michael Landon's Power Key of Miracles

**TRUTH**

Truth is the essence of listening to the inner self
Reflect often on the important priorities of life
Understand that miracles do take place in an instant
Tell others how much they mean to you daily
Harvest the sweet blessed parts of life and cherish them

### Michael Landon's Miracle Visualization

Allow 10 minutes for this entire process or more as desired. Breathe in for 8 counts, hold 8 counts and release 8 counts. Envision a bright emerald green waterfall flowing down through the top of your head through to your feet and into the center of the earth. As you breathe in, allow the waterfall to become more concentrated until you feel full saturation within every cell of your being, nervous system, circulatory system, muscular system and structural system. Ask for the total healing of every cell on every level and dimension of your being, especially in weak areas of the body. Affirm the absolute perfection of health spiritually, emotionally, mentally, and physically. Begin to notice your body becoming stronger and fortified in the bright emerald green fountains. Feel the presence of Archangel Raphael working with you. Send the healing radiance out to loved ones, friends and the entire world, seeing all brought back into perfect balance. Clasp your hands together at the end and affirm, it is done, and so it is.

AFFIRMATION: I AM MIRACLES ON ALL LEVELS FOREVER.

*Miracles to All in All Ways,*
*Michael Landon (Kalia)*

# Chapter 13

## *Afterlife Wisdom of Mahatma Gandhi*

### **Connection with Mahatma Gandhi in Spirit**

The communication with Mahatma Gandhi has been at very special times when I have been chanting or meditating, and at times when I have been near statues or pictures of him. His beautiful wisdom and peaceful presence always calms one; he usually appears in a golden robe (symbolizing wisdom), and his presence is always profound. These discourses convey his messages of truth and wisdom for the key to peaceful resolutions for all of humanity. It is indeed an honor and privilege to present them.

Mahatma Gandhi's Discourses - Peaceful Resolutions

Q. Now that you know what you know, what would you have done differently in your life?
A. My life was a magnificent role well played and at the end I ascended back into the realms of the golden light. If I were to change anything, I would have done even more to assist humanity in realizing its own eternal life and divinity.

Q. What is your mission in the afterlife?
A. My mission continues in the order of the Golden Robe (Peace) to extend golden light as an emissary to global leaders and to help all humanity realize its highest potential. My role here as it was on earth is to dispel the darkness created by ignorance of universal laws. I work to restore the dignity and integrity of global leaders, politicians,

and peacemakers along with many other beings. We cannot interfere with free will, but special dispensations are now in order for us to intervene in matters where truth, justice and peace are threatened. All is protected and all is well. I extend the golden chalice out to humanity as a message that all is in attunement with the golden sun within them. I am in the order of the golden light, which is infinite wisdom and peace. I take all into the garden of victory here to be aligned in the highest way. In these realms my mission as a teacher and spiritual leader continues. I, along with many others, bring forth infinite wisdom into all hearts and minds. In these realms, I also work with many world leaders to assist them in shifting to higher wisdom for their decisions and actions. Much of the cause and effects of humanity's actions are now becoming evident and all are being raised to new levels for greater understanding. The universal law of free will plays a part in humanity's choices, but the group consciousness on earth is choosing peace.

I send my unending love and devotion to all that they may feel my presence within their hearts.

Q. What is your message for the world?

A. The full integration of east and west philosophies is now at hand on earth and this is a beautiful thing as a deeper understanding for the spiritual path will take place. I too assist in programs for higher universal education for the young ones that they may learn to go within for their true answers and find the inner strength and confidence in themselves. Many young children are intended to be great world leaders. Listen to the young ones for they have great wisdom to share.

I work to assist the masses in the full raising of the vibrations on the earth plane. We here have our own form of "summit" to assist in the great changes for world peace, harmony, wellness and balance. There are millions now holding the vision for the new template of the planet and mother earth is cleaning her surfaces to prepare for the grand new world. The outcome of the darkness (shadow) and the light must play itself out and in the end the divine plan for truth and justice is indeed fulfilled. Remember to hold on to the golden chalice I send forth to all today within your heart, for it encompasses all that is needed for soul evolvement, clearing of obstacles, wellness, wealth, joy and compassion. With these elements, all is possible.

This is the time of the great cleansing of old archaic ideas and thought forms. It is the Golden Renaissance.

**Q. What is the true key to Peace?**

A. The principle of peace is within the Self. Find peace deep within your heart center. It matters not whether one is a prince or pauper, a king or a peasant, peace is within the self and it ignites all manifestation. The great sages and saints of all time to infinity have known and fought for the secrets of the universal pathways. Yet all have come to know and to understand what is called the great "All That Is," and that they are one within that universal light. They have come to know the importance of all they do, every task, every word, every thought as it is done in pure golden grace, humility, reverence, love, compassion, understanding, attunement, fortitude and oneness.

The secret of true peace lies in that great silence within the Self in All That Is. For, in truth, nothing else exists. All else is but shadow. And so it is in the radiance of these spheres of golden grace we come unto you, showering you and lifting you into these spheres that you might know and feel and remember - you are the golden grace.

When one comes back to the focus of the golden grace in attunement and alignment of all bodies of the cellular structure and the soul structure– the physical structure, the mental structure, emotional structure, all levels, all dimensions, all time, all space–there is only the one knowing. And in this, all answers come, all decisions, all creation. In the holding of the chalice of golden grace within your own heart of hearts, it can be extended out to all others–your beloved ones and all beloved ones throughout all humanity, throughout this entire planet and galaxy. In this way, the golden chalice of peace and grace shall be sustained through all time.

I, that one known as Gandhi, representing the golden spheres of light, the golden radiance, come unto you this day and remind you that YOU ARE THE PEACE THAT YOU SEEK, AND HAVE ALWAYS BEEN. Extend your hand to your brother and to your sister. Surround each day, each one you meet with reverence. For it is in that gentleness and kindness of the great silence–that gentleness and kindness that also was brought forth by that beloved one known as Jesus the Christ when he walked upon the Earth – it is in that loving radiance that all peace is created within and around.

### Mahatma Gandhi's Power Key of Peaceful Resolutions

PEACE
Prepare yourself for Enlightenment
Elevate your compassion for humanity
Allow the highest and best solutions for challenges
Change injustice to justice with forgiveness and persistence
Engage in peaceful resolutions everyday for win-win

### Mahatma Gandhi's World Peace Visualization

Relax into a gentle meditation breathing in nine counts, holding nine counts and releasing nine counts throughout the visualization (10 minutes). Begin to envision the golden sun beaming through every cell of your being, warming you and relaxing every part of your body. Let the golden pillar of light extend through you into the center of the earth below you and spiral back up to the heavens. See a golden archway connecting the entire country, continents and planet in a golden dome. Send this dome of peace to all of humanity and envision them looking up with peace and happiness in their hearts. See the entirety of humanity now joining hands in the golden dome chanting 10 times "Om Namah Shivaya" (I honor the Divine within). I leave you with this message: hold the entire planet in the golden chalice of infinite wisdom, love and power within your heart of hearts. Watch the world accelerate in its change to the grand new world of true peace, freedom and harmony for all. My blessings unto all on behalf of the Order of the Golden Light. And so it is, "Let there be peace on earth." May Eternal Love and Peace be with you always.

AFFIRMATION: PEACEFUL RESOLUTIONS ARE NOW REALITY

*Namaste,*
*Mahatma Gandhi*

# Chapter 14

## *Afterlife Wisdom of Mother Theresa*

### *Connection with Mother Theresa in Spirit*

Mother Theresa first started appearing to me within a year after her passing at times when I needed extra encouragement on my path and in my life. She comes into my meditations especially at times when I need confirmation and inspiration for my work. She usually appears in a beautiful opal-essence crystalline robe with crown on her head (symbolizing transfiguration and ascension). Her prayers remain profound and powerful for all who call upon her. Her key for a compassionate world is powerful in her beautiful discourses herein. She, too, is a member of the Order of the Rose (Compassion) with Princess Diana and many others. May you feel her nurturing and inspiring presence through her messages.

Mother Theresa's Discourses - Compassionate World

Q. What is your mission in the celestial realms?
A. I come to you this day, as a mother would nurture her children. My mission for assisting humanity continues here in these realms as it was on earth. I work in the Legions of the Opal Essence, which is the legion of transfiguration and ascension. I also work in the Order of the Rose (Compassion). I work with multiple color rays and my focus is devotion to healing and assisting those who call out to be uplifted and inspired. We come forth to send the message to all to open their hearts to more  charitable deeds. Rather than being a

doormat, actively assist the many thousands of souls who are less fortunate to create justice and harmony.

We see many leaders who are still in a selfish role of "me first." I come to you through these brief messages to let all know that this work continues in these spheres of light and we work for the transfiguration of all humanity, raising their vibrations so they may know their soul purpose in this lifetime.

**Q. What is your message for the world?**

A. In reality, there is only one truth. Many denominations, many faiths, many religions, but only one truth.

We work in these spheres of light through transfiguration to purify and blend the discrimination and the discrepancies of a vast number of religions who fight among each other–casting in thoughts, words and actions hatred, envy, misunderstanding, defense and often wars and killing. Through the centuries, many battles have been fought over faith or over religion. The ethnocentric ego self really truly knows nothing of higher truth.

If all can see clearly that there is only one source, one higher truth, and honor the grains of truth within all creeds and all religions, then there is a blend of multicultural faith. We see great strides as we have been working in these realms to create groups and organizations to focus exactly on this– interdenominational, interfaith communities where all cultures, all faiths come together.

This we see as a beautiful rose unfolding within the hearts of humanity. This is our prayer indeed, as the summit of all world spiritual leaders call a summit of all humanity to be together in honor and understanding, for there is much to learn from each other.

Therefore, we are working diligently from these spheres of light through the ray of transfiguration to purify the planet. When all are united in knowing and honoring the one source, one universe of light and all as one consciousness evolving, all is pure divine love. The frequency of that pure plane of love knows no limits, no boundaries. For within this sphere of pure divine radiance of love, there is all creation.

As humanity reaches much higher levels of knowing and understanding, they will see the superfluous nature of the past, where individuals and nations fought against each other, tore each other down, decided that one is more right than the other. This is truly an illusion. Know that all are one, all are equal, all are united in the universal light–Buddhist, Hindu, Muslim, Christian, all faiths, all creeds and races. There is no separation–only that created with the human mind.

Q. If you knew what you know now, how would you have lived life differently?

A. I would have continued to do my humanitarian work in service as a teacher to open hearts of humanity and I would have continued in the service of the Light in an even grander way for all souls. The essence of Divine Masculine and Feminine is what we aspire to integrate in all of humanity and this is not an easy task as the consciousness is still confined in old ways of thinking. Overall, the Blueprint is changing. Men are often as little boys who only need love, tenderness and compassion. They often close down communication and rule solely with the mind. There are many great Spiritual leaders and teachers now that will raise them into their own true essence and power.

Women are now coming into their true power to be independent and focus on their life endeavors. This shift is taking place throughout humanity and the US is a template for change. Men are realizing they need to come into true balance of male/female energy; they are seeing that there is a shift and they can no longer dominate others in this defense of their own weaknesses. We smile as we watch these occurrences on earth as we are focused to mold this into a balance of true love, power and wisdom - pink, symbolizing divine love, symbolizing blue divine power, and gold, symbolizing divine wisdom. These three colors bring forth a full balance within the heart (the 3-fold flame). We are here to assist all to know their true purpose in this lifetime and the reality that there is only one Truth.

I would have continued to do my humanitarian work in service as a teacher to open hearts of humanity and I would have continued in the service of the Light in an even grander way for all souls. I would have called forth the greater organizing of this work, for I had the power to do this in alignment with people in positions of power. I see now I could have done even more on a broader scale, so I do it from these realms through others who follow in my work.

Overall I had a mission and example to present, I achieved it, and for this I have a special place in the heavenly realms where I am at peace and continue this work with many others, Princess Diana included - as she is my sister of light.

### Mother Theresa's Power Key to a Compassionate World

COMPASSION
Cleanse all prejudice and discrimination
Open to greater understanding of all others
Minimize the suffering through Selfless Service
Prepare children by teaching them equality
Allow Injustice to become Justice
See a vision of Peace through Forgiveness
Serve all in a humanitarian way
Ignite the Love, Power & Wisdom within
Offer solutions to the world's problems
Now is the time for a Compassionate World

### Mother Theresa's World Compassion Visualization

Breathe in for eight counts, hold for eight counts and release eight counts in a cyclical breathing process throughout the visualization (20 minutes long). Visualize a beautiful crystalline opal essence star above you (filled with rainbow light). Let the star beam through you, filling every cell within your crown, head, throat, heart, solar plexus, abdomen, base and legs with the radiant crystalline opal essence of light flooding you. Let this starlight beam through you into the center of the earth, where it links with the heart center of the earth. Allow this radiance to ignite with the entire world as you go more deeply into meditation. This radiance is now transcending all past bringing all into balance within you on every level. Begin to envision a pink flame, blue flame and golden flame of light (3-Fold Flame), beam through into your heart center, blending as one (love, power and wisdom). Feel your entire being come into full balance and extend the 3-fold flame to envelop the entire planet. Visualize billions of people opening their hearts to Compassion for one another and helping, sharing, uniting as one. See all past hatred and injustices dissolve. Envision all of humanity enveloped in Opal Essence starlight.

## AFFIRMATION: MIRACLES OF COMPASSION NOW FILL THE WORLD

*Dear one, may the perpetual light of Forgiveness, Compassion & Grace be within your heart of hearts.. May a thousand rose petals fall upon you ever so lightly to lift and enlighten you. "We" are with you always ...*

*My unending Love and Blessings,*
*Mother Theresa*

## Color Chart Of Ray Of Lights

**Princess Diana:** *Prik/Magenta* - Love & Compassion

**Elvis:** *Blue* - Will, Faith & Communications

**Jackie O. Kennedy:** *Violet* - Liberty/Freedom

**John F. Kennedy:** *Violet* - Justice & Freedom

**Martin Luther King:** *Violet* - Freedom

**Johnny Carson:** *Yellow/Gold* - Creativity & Wisdom

**Judy Garland:** *White/Ruby* - Purification & Power

**John Lennon:** Yellow - Creativity & Arts

**Howard Hughes:** *Gold* - Wisdom & Prosperity

**Princess Grace:** *Aquamarine* - Clarity & Serenity

**Michael Landon:** *Green* - Healing & Truth

**Elizabeth Montgomery:** *Peach* - Enthusiasm/Joy

**Gandhi:** *Gold* - Wisdom & Peace

**Mother Theresa:** *Opal Essence* - Transfiguration/All that Is

## *Join The Celebrities In Spirit Wisdom Club!*

# Testimonials

*"Athena has an amazing gift!! After the insights that I recieved from her session I was able to make some changes that I know changed the course of my life for the better. I will be eternally grateful!!!"*

Monique Edwards, TV/Screen Actor

*"I experienced an awesome change at a deep level from working with Athena, which has transformed my life and business."*

(R Lothomer, Bus. Owner, OR)

*"After taking Athena's TeleConfs, I experienced major breakthrus in my persona and career goals shortly thereafter."*

(C Daly, VA)

*"The weekly teleseminars are so very powerful and so personal, I feel very blessed to have been a part of it."*

(S Mayes, Business Owner, TX)

*"An outstanding book! I am left feeling inspired, more creative and able to trust my inner wisdom and ability to accomplish all I desire."* Ntathu Allen, Yoga Teacher and author 'Returning Home to the Healing Waters of my Soul'

*"A very enlightening and inspirational book recommended as a daily reference."* Acayasha, Author & Radio Host

## *About the Author*

AthenaStar has been a Visionary Consultant, Teacher & Spiritual Messenger for 20 years and has a Master's Degree in Human Resources from Central Michigan University with several years experience in Personnel Mangement. As an ordained minister, she is also a Reiki Master Healer and has acquired holistic/esoteric training through various spiritual foundations and mystery school teachings. Working with thousands of clients worldwide, she has given life-transformational sessions, seminars and tele-seminars for personal and career success, empowerment, prosperity, relationships, and spiritual development. In addition to assisting dignitaries, corporate officials and world teachers, she has hosted local TV and radio Talk Shows in Hawaii and is a frequent national Radio/TV guest. Her articles are published in many national motivational magazines and ezines. Athena provides transformational consulting services both in person and long distance by phone to create wellness and success. She is available for professional speaking, workshops and media interviews internationally.

**athenastar.com or 808 258 1063**

Lightning Source UK Ltd.
Milton Keynes UK
UKHW010521150420
361682UK00005BA/1642